HAPPY JESUS

Other Books By Bear Jack Gebhardt

(See them all on Amazon.com)

Practicing the Presence of Peace

How to Stop Smoking in 15 Easy Years
  A Slacker's Guide to Final Freedom

The Enlightened Smoker' Guide to Quitting

How to Help Your Smoker Quit

Now Hiring (with Steve Lauer)

Happy Jesus

Local Boy Makes Good!
An Advaita Gospel

Bear Jack Gebhardt

Seven Traditions Press
Fort Collins, Colorado

Copyright © 2012 by Bear Jack Gebhardt

All rights reserved. Published 2012

First Edition

ISBN: 13: 978-1938651038

Printed in the United States of America

TO FREE THINKERS EVERYWHERE

And especially to Clarence Jordon, author of *Cotton Patch Gospels*, who showed me it could be done, and to my older brother Bob

Who carries on the tradition with deep wisdom, compassion and insight

THANKS FOR LEADING THE WAY.

Introduction

How Happy Jesus Came To Be

*"G*od told me I should break the human law," a new friend told me, in the privacy of my cabin, high in the Colorado mountains. I nodded my head. She was an intelligent, well-educated, well-traveled middle-aged woman who was sharing confidences by a warm fire. I'm the senior librarian at Heart Mountain Monastery so people sometimes come to me with problems, or confessions or just good stories they want to share.

"If the authorities discovered what I did," she continued. "I know I would go to prison, either here in America or in Israel. Or first here and then there."

Again I nodded my head, accepting her confession, her story. "But even if I should end up in prison," she said, "It would be worth it, because I have no doubt whatsoever that God told me to do it."

Little warning signs, of course, went off in my head. We were on dangerous ground. Some of the most horrific crimes, both personal and communal, in both ancient and modern history have been excused on the grounds that "God told me to do it." This lady might be wacko. As Teresa of Avila had warned, if God tells you to do anything, you are absolutely not to do it. Rather, go immediately to your priest and make your confession.

We've matured since Teresa's time, of course, but still, one must be cautious.

The thin, bright-eyed little lady sitting with me in my cabin smiled at me patiently as we sat in the quiet of the crackling fire. As mentioned, she was a new friend, had been attending various events at Heart Mountain

Monastery for several months. I didn't know her well but what I did know of her I enjoyed and was impressed. She was a Cambridge trained Biblical scholar, able to read and speak Ancient Hebrew, Greek and Aramaic.

She had taken me aside one morning after a meditation class that I had been teaching. She asked for an appointment to talk privately. As the senior librarian for our monastery I had assumed she wanted to have access to some of our rarer books—no problem-- or discuss some aspect of scripture or spiritual practice. Though I love books, and especially spiritual books from every culture, and have spent my life pouring through them, I'm much more a cowboy-monk-librarian than an academic scholar, so I was a little worried that I would quickly be in over my head with this Cambridge trained intellectual.

Now, here in my cabin, shortly after pouring our tea, other possibilities of what she needed were going through my mind. Still, I was not ready for what she said next.

"And I'm also just as certain," she said, "that God told me that you, Bear, would help me get away with my little crime, and help me finish this project." She smiled.

Oh-oh. Now I knew she was wacko.

I smiled back, nodded my head. "Must be nice to have a private line to God," I said.

She laughed. That was a good sign. "I know what you're thinking," she said. "You're thinking I'm wacko."

As mentioned, that's *exactly* what I'd been thinking. That she used my own particular private thought-word for it was a bit unnerving.

"Let me just tell it to you straight," she said. "I smuggled out of Israel and into the United States, in a sealed, temperature controlled chamber, an early edition of the Gospel of John."

I looked at her and nodded my head, as if I understood.

"In fact," she went on, "it may be the earliest edition ever discovered of the Gospel of John. During my stay here at Heart Mountain, I have been able to complete my translation. The Abbot knows what I've been doing. The ancient text is wonderful. And it's revolutionary. And I want you to publish it, and do so under your own name. The Abbot has given me permission to ask you, though he says it's your choice as to whether you accept."

"I don't understand," I said.

"You don't have to say yes or no until after you've read the manuscript," she said.

"But why all the secrecy?" I asked.

"Because even though this is a very simple text, it challenges church orthodoxy in fundamental ways. Whoever's name is on it when it is published could be the target of much public criticism and even anger."

"Thanks," I said "That's what I've been looking for."

She laughed. "I think that's why the Abbot said you would be the one to do it," she replied.

"Actually, public criticism is not my forte, " I said. "But tell me, what's so different about your version?"

"Read it and see," she said. She leaned down next to her chair, picked up her large bag and drew out a blue folder. The blue folder contained a neatly stacked bundle of pages. She handed the folder to me. I still remember that first exchange of papers, there in my cabin by the firelight. Looking back, it's as if I had been given a ball of light, as Ezra Pound might say.

As she handed me the folder, she said, "In this translation of the earliest version of John, we are *all* the sons and daughters of God. Not just Jesus. According to this text, that's what Jesus came to teach. That we are all sons and daughters of God. It was only in the later editions—the ones that were changed—that made Jesus the one and only."

We were both quiet for a long moment. "Those versions seemed to have worked pretty well for a lot of people over the past couple of thousand years," I observed, holding the blue folder in my lap. .

"Yes, yes of course, they work if you can read between the lines," she said. "His teaching is there, for anyone to see. But how many can read between the lines? And how many think it's a sin or are taught that it's a sin to read between the lines?"

I didn't answer.

"He came to teach peace on earth," she went on. "He said—even in the King James version he said—I have come that my joy might be in you and that your joy might be full. Are we peaceful yet? Is our joy full?"

"For many Christians, yes," I said. "Their joy *is* full. Their peace *is* deep."

Although in my own spiritual practice I'm a fairly eclectic fellow—make that a radically eclectic fellow--- I am not into Christian bashing.

She nodded her head in agreement, smiled at me and took a deep breath. In a much quieter tone she said, "I am a practicing Christian. I love the Bible. It's my lifeline.

Introduction: How Happy Jesus Came to Be……………………………..v

It's my life. Even the old King James version. I love it. The spirit of Christ runs through it. Anyone who picks it up can sense that spirit, if they earnestly look for it, and are open to it. I'm not arguing that.

"Yet you yourself have talked in your classes about the changes that have been made to the Bible down through the centuries. And small changes continue to be made, first here, then there, some official, some by a single monk in his cell copying manuscripts. Some of the changes were accidental. Others were made to better conform to some particular church orthodoxy. The manuscript that you are holding is the Book of John in its earliest form, the earliest one ever discovered. It's what was there before the orthodoxy was put in, before the mistakes were made. Aren't you curious?" Her eyes sparkled.

"Yes of course I'm curious," I said, looking at the manuscript in my lap. "Where did you get it?"

She shook her head. "No, no. That's why I need a third party to publish it. That's why I've come to you. If I told you where I got it, and how, I assure you that you, too, would be complicit in breaking the Israeli Antiquities Law and the International Antiquities Law and half a dozen other laws. My intent is to return the original manuscript after we have translated it and arranged for publication. Do you know how long it took for the original Dead Sea Scrolls to be released to the public?"

"A long time, as I remember."

"Some of them are *still* not released," she said. "Even after sixty years! This can't wait sixty years."

I was quiet.

"So just read it," she said. "See if you like it. See if it works for you. If it does, I would be honored if you would publish it under your name."

"Thank you for your trust," I said. "I will read it, and let you know."

"That's all I ask," she said, and stood up to leave. "If you aren't moved to do it, that means you aren't the right one for it. It would be foolish of me to ask you to do something that you were not happy to do, that your own peace did not inspire you to do."

So of course I read the manuscript. I started that night, and finished reading it the next day. The fact that you are now holding it in your hand should tell you about my immediate and enthusiastic response to her request that I publish it under my own name.

Yet I can't and don't take credit for it. The credit goes, first, of course, to Jesus himself, for teaching us this simple way of life, and giving us demonstration after demonstration as to how it works. And then the credit goes to John, back in A.D. 70, who wrote down the stories, that we can all learn and know this way. And then the credit goes to all the countless, anonymous millions who practiced the way day by day over thousands of years to keep the flame alive, keep the teaching alive, so that we might have it here in the age of twitter, space ships and cell phones. And finally, the credit goes to not only my new friend who risked her life to bring this to us, but to all those countless others who translated it down through the years, into their own language, into every language on the planet, according to their own lights, often at the risk of imprisonment, exile or death.. All of these translators, lovers of the Bible, were and are so brave, and so inspired. We owe them our lives.

Thank you, all, for all of this.

Bear Jack Gebhardt,
Senior Librarian
Heart Mountain Monastery.

These things have I spoken unto you,
that my joy might remain in you,
and that your joy might be full.

John 15-11

Chapter One

(King James version)

In the beginning was the Word, and the Word was with God, and the Word was God.

²The same was in the beginning with God.

³All things were made by him; and without him was not any thing made that was made.

⁴In him was life; and the life was the light of men.

⁵And the light shineth in darkness; and the darkness comprehended it not.

⁶There was a man sent from God, whose name *was* John.

⁷·The same came for a witness, to bear witness of the Light, that all *men* through him might believe.

⁸He was not that Light, but *was sent* to bear witness of that Light.

⁹· *That* was the true Light, which lighteth every man that cometh into the world.

Chapter One

1. In the beginning was Joy; alive, aware, intelligent and still. This objectless Joy, this Happiness, this Awareness was and is the first Word of God.

2. These words, *Joy, Happiness, Awareness, God*, point to the same wordless, divine Presence.

3. All things arise out of joy and return to joy, this divinely happy aware Presence.

4. Joy is the essence of all existence, and thus joy is the essence of being human, of humans being.

5. Although this aware-joy is always present, both within and without, sometimes we humans remember joy and, being human, sometimes we forget.

6. John the Baptist had learned, in his way and in his time, to remember to listen to his joy, and thus he could confidently speak of joy to others.

7. John's remembering and listening to joy and then speaking of joy to others was meant simply to encourage and inspire others to likewise remember their own joy and listen to it in their own way and in their own time.

8. Joy itself is timeless, formless, endless. This speaking of joy in our own time and in our own way is not the joy itself but rather a particular and unique time and space expression of joy.

9. A new expression of joy occurs again every time a baby is born. And throughout the baby's life, from childhood to old age, joy itself is available as essence, and thus as the navigational beacon to guide the child's way in absolutely every time and place and relationship and circumstance.

[10] He was in the world, and the world was made by him, and the world knew him not.

[11] He came unto his own, and his own received him not.

[12] But as many as received him, to them gave he power to become the sons of God, *even* to them that believe on his name:

[13] Which were born, not of blood, nor of the will of the flesh, nor of the will of man, but of God.

[14] And the Word was made flesh, and dwelt among us, (and we beheld his glory, the glory as of the only begotten of the Father,) full of grace and truth.

[15] John bare witness of him, and cried, saying, This was he of whom I spake, He that cometh after me is preferred before me: for he was before me.

[16] And of his fulness have all we received, and grace for grace.

[17] For the law was given by Moses, *but* grace and truth came by Jesus Christ.

10. The same aware joy that made the universe is the aware joy that is in our hearts. It is a single awareness, a single joy.

11. Too often, because of lack of training and cultural ignorance, we forget or neglect the intelligent happiness that is already here, in each of our hearts. We overlook or ignore the easy joy that is closer than our breath.

12. But we *can* remember, we *can* return our attention to our innate, abiding happiness, time and time again, and when we do, our lives are illumined; our lives blossom; we move by grace; peace returns, as does healing and prosperity, for ourselves and all those around us.

13. When we return our attention to happiness itself we discover it is already everywhere present; Joy is our inheritance, our namesake, so that we no longer need to struggle and war with the three-dimensional world, attempting to arrange and rearrange its people and pieces in order to *force* happiness to occur. We were born into it.

14. Jesus is our exemplar. He showed us our potential, the astounding grace, the full radiance and power of joy when it is given its rightful reign in our human form.

15. John the Baptist recognized that Jesus was giving full expression to the Undying Joy that is in the heart of every human. "There," John said, when he first saw Jesus, "That's the joy I've been speaking about, that I've been pointing to. This man knows the joy that was here before all of us, and that leads us each to our own inheritance. It's this man's expression of joy that we all can follow.

16. "His presence here shows us our joyful inheritance. Jesus shows us it can be done, and what it looks like.

17. "The deep potential of complete joy has been pointed to before, and given human structure and permanence by men such as Moses. Jesus now shows us how such complete joy actually functions here in our everyday world.

¹⁸No man hath seen God at any time; the only begotten Son, which is in the bosom of the Father, he hath declared *him*.

¹⁹And this is the record of John, when the Jews sent priests and Levites from Jerusalem to ask him, Who art thou?

²⁰And he confessed, and denied not; but confessed, I am not the Christ.

²¹And they asked him, What then? Art thou Elias? And he saith, I am not. Art thou that prophet? And he answered, No.

²²Then said they unto him, Who art thou? that we may give an answer to them that sent us. What sayest thou of thyself?

²³He said, I *am* the voice of one crying in the wilderness, Make straight the way of the Lord, as said the prophet Esaias.

²⁴And they which were sent were of the Pharisees.

²⁵And they asked him, and said unto him, Why baptizest thou then, if thou be not that Christ, nor Elias, neither that prophet?

²⁶John answered them, saying, I baptize with water: but there standeth one among you, whom ye know not;

18. "None of us can actually see happiness, or joy with our physical eyes, or hear it with our ears, or feel it with our hands or taste it with our tongue, and yet it is here, in the very depths of the atomic structure. This joy is prior to and beyond the sense impressions. It lies at the heart of the universe itself. This is the joy that Jesus shows us."

19. For the people of his time John the Baptist was a powerful spokesman, and continually pointed to the underlying, aware-joy at the heart of the universe.

20. Nevertheless, John made it very clear to those who asked that his own experience and expression of the ancient joy was still incomplete and partial.

21. The people then complained that if John's experience of joy was still incomplete, then before he could talk about it he needed some kind of authority other than the authority of joy. But John said no, that he needed no other authority than joy.

22. They pressed him on the issue: how could he teach about joy the way he was doing, if he himself was not the master of joy? What was his role? What was he doing?

23. John replied that he was simply introducing people to joy, pointing to joy, even if those around him were reluctant to look to where he was pointing. He said that joy has always been at the heart of life and that many others before him had pointed to the exact same thing.

24. Most of the people who were listening to him were very traditional.

25. "Since you don't have any real authority to teach joy, or to introduce people to joy, why do you do it?" the people continued to ask.

26. "I just introduce the basics of joy," John said, "the bare minimum. But another man has come here now to teach us the fullness of joy, even though you folks haven't recognized him yet.

[27] He it is, who coming after me is preferred before me, whose shoe's latchet I am not worthy to unloose.

[8] These things were done in Bethabara beyond Jordan, where John was baptizing.

[29] The next day John seeth Jesus coming unto him, and saith, Behold the Lamb of God, which taketh away the sin of the world.

[30] This is he of whom I said, After me cometh a man which is preferred before me: for he was before me.

[31] And I knew him not: but that he should be made manifest to Israel, therefore am I come baptizing with water.

[32] And John bare record, saying, I saw the Spirit descending from heaven like a dove, and it abode upon him.

[33] And I knew him not: but he that sent me to baptize with water, the same said unto me, Upon whom thou shalt see the Spirit descending, and remaining on him, the same is he which baptizeth with the Holy Ghost.

[34] And I saw, and bare record that this is the Son of God.

27. "My own simple introductions and teachings about joy don't have one tenth the insight and power of the teachings and demonstrations of the one you're about to meet. Compared to his sunlight, my joy is a candle."

28. John was saying these things to the local people when they had gathered at the edge of town, down by the river.

29. The next day, at the same place, John saw Jesus walking toward him. "There, that's the guy," John said. "He's the one I was talking about yesterday. He's the one who can show anybody in the world how to dissolve any unhappiness. He is pure joy itself, awareness itself.

30. "Most of us identify ourselves with the human flesh that is born and dies, that comes and goes, but this guy is identified with joy, with awareness itself, which never dies, that is here both before and after all that appears and disappears. He is the one we can all learn from.

31. "I talk about joy, I point to joy, but I've not yet learned to fully identify with it. But this guy is joy itself. He's the one who can show us and the whole world how it's done.

32. "Joy is within each of us," John said, "and now Jesus is showing us what the joy inside looks like when it is fully manifest, from inside to outside. He is so at peace with himself and the world that I saw a dove come and sit on his shoulder. This is what heaven on earth looks like.

33. "In the past I have encouraged people to look within for their joy, but I was not able to fully demonstrate joy, to give people an actual experience of joy. But this man Jesus can do that. When you put your attention on Jesus you are putting your attention on the universal joy. This is the joy that was here even before the world was here. This man is an expression of the first power.

34. "So we can all rest now and be both glad and confident that we now know what the eternal joy behind the universe itself looks like, and feels like when it is fully expressed here in its human form."

³⁵Again the next day after John stood, and two of his disciples;

³⁶And looking upon Jesus as he walked, he saith, Behold the Lamb of God!

³⁷And the two disciples heard him speak, and they followed Jesus.

³⁸Then Jesus turned, and saw them following, and saith unto them, What seek ye? They said unto him, Rabbi, (which is to say, being interpreted, Master,) where dwellest thou?

³⁹He saith unto them, Come and see. They came and saw where he dwelt, and abode with him that day: for it was about the tenth hour.

⁴⁰One of the two which heard John *speak*, and followed him, was Andrew, Simon Peter's brother.

⁴¹He first findeth his own brother Simon, and saith unto him, We have found the Messias, which is, being interpreted, the Christ.

⁴²And he brought him to Jesus. And when Jesus beheld him, he said, Thou art Simon the son of Jona: thou shalt be called Cephas, which is by interpretation, A stone.

⁴³The day following Jesus would go forth into Galilee, and findeth Philip, and saith unto him, Follow me.

In the Beginning Was Joy

³⁵. This is what John the Baptist said to several close friends at a particular time and place after he saw Jesus. And the next day John saw Jesus again.

³⁶. "There he is again," John said. "That's the man whose job is to bring a new awareness of joy to earth, and who will show the world how to drop all its unhappiness."

³⁷. John's two friends could sense that John was telling the truth, and so they naturally went to be with Jesus.

³⁸. And when Jesus saw John's friends approaching he turned and asked them, "What are you looking for?" "A teacher," they said. "Are you the one? Where do you come from? How do you teach the way that you do? What is going on there inside of you?"

³⁹. Jesus smiled. "Just come along. Hang out with me for a while, and I'll show you." And so the two friends of John went with Jesus, and began to feel his happiness and understand what he was all about. This was early in Jesus' teaching career.

⁴⁰. One of these friends who went that day with Jesus was Andrew, who we now know as Jesus' first disciple. Andrew's brother was Simon Peter.

⁴¹. Andrew told Simon, "We have found the teacher we've been looking for without even knowing we were looking. This guy really does know what happiness is all about. And he's willing to help *everybody* figure it out."

⁴². So Andrew took his brother to see Jesus, and when Jesus saw Simon Peter Jesus quickly recognized him as someone who would help him bring joy to the whole world. "Hello Simon," Jesus said, calling him by name without being introduced. "You and I are going to be great friends. You're a very solid and honest man."

⁴³. The next day Jesus went to a neighboring town to meet another friend, named Phillip, who would also help out with the work that Jesus was putting together. When he

⁴⁴Now Philip was of Bethsaida, the city of Andrew and Peter.

⁴⁵Philip findeth Nathanael, and saith unto him, We have found him, of whom Moses in the law, and the prophets, did write, Jesus of Nazareth, the son of Joseph.

⁴⁶And Nathanael said unto him, Can there any good thing come out of Nazareth? Philip saith unto him, Come and see.

⁴⁷Jesus saw Nathanael coming to him, and saith of him, Behold an Israelite indeed, in whom is no guile!

⁴⁸Nathanael saith unto him, Whence knowest thou me? Jesus answered and said unto him, Before that Philip called thee, when thou wast under the fig tree, I saw thee.

⁴⁹Nathanael answered and saith unto him, Rabbi, thou art the Son of God; thou art the King of Israel.

⁵⁰Jesus answered and said unto him, Because I said unto thee, I saw thee under the fig tree, believest thou? thou shalt see greater things than these.

⁵¹And he saith unto him, Verily, verily, I say unto you, Hereafter ye shall see heaven open, and the angels of God ascending and descending upon the Son of man.

saw Phillip, he said, "Come on, friend. Follow me. We've all got some happy work to do here shortly."

44. It was no coincidence that Phillip and Andrew and Peter all grew up in the same town.

45. Phillip then went to his friend Nathaniel to tell him about what was happening. "We've found the teacher we've all been waiting for without knowing we were waiting," he said to Nathaniel. "He's the son of a carpenter, from Nazareth, and just like the scriptures said could happen, this guy knows what happiness is all about. Being with him is like heaven on earth."

46. "He's from Nazareth?" Nathaniel said. "That podunk town? What could he have learned in Nazareth that we don't already know here?" "Just come with me," Phillip said. "You'll see."

47. So Nathaniel went with Phillip and when Jesus saw Nathaniel Jesus said, "Here comes a dude from Israel who talks honest, and likes to call a spade a spade."

48. This surprised Nathaniel. "How do you know where I'm from, and what I'm like?" Jesus replied, "I heard what you said when you were talking with Phillip, there under the tree. Happiness has no boundaries of time or space."

49. Nathaniel was convinced. "You got me, sir," Nathaniel said. "Apparently, you *do* know what happiness is all about. I think you are going to be our *go-to* guy."

50. Jesus laughed. "You're an easy sale," he said. "Just because joy led me to see you there under the tree, you're sold. My new friend, you haven't seen anything yet."

51. "When you know joy, you'll know the workings of the universe. Joy quickens every expression at every level of existence and because of joy every level works gracefully together, both coming and going. Joy reveals the

Chapter Two

¹And the third day there was a marriage in Cana of Galilee; and the mother of Jesus was there:

²And both Jesus was called, and his disciples, to the marriage.

³And when they wanted wine, the mother of Jesus saith unto him, They have no wine.

⁴Jesus saith unto her, Woman, what have I to do with thee? mine hour is not yet come.

⁵His mother saith unto the servants, Whatsoever he saith unto you, do *it*.

⁶And there were set there six waterpots of stone, after the manner of the purifying of the Jews, containing two or three firkins apiece.

⁷Jesus saith unto them, Fill the waterpots with water. And they filled them up to the brim.

⁸And he saith unto them, Draw out now, and bear unto the governor of the feast. And they bare *it*.

⁹When the ruler of the feast had tasted the water that was made wine, and knew not whence it was: (but the servants which drew the water knew;) the governor of the feast called the bridegroom,

innate harmony that breathes, supports and animates every form and helps everything on earth to evolve."

Chapter Two

1. That same week Jesus' mother was planning to attend a fancy marriage in a neighboring town.

2. When the hosts found out that Jesus was also going to be around, he sent an invitation to Jesus and Andrew and Peter and several other of Jesus' new friends.

3. . After the ceremony, at the reception, when people had been drinking for a while, Jesus' mom came to him and told him that the hosts had run out of wine.

4. Jesus laughed. "Mom, you're pushing me," he said. "When I'm ready to go public, I'll let you know."

5. His mom smiled, shrugged her shoulders and turned to some of the help who were there to serve at the wedding. "This man's in charge," she said. "Please help him, if he should ask, and just do whatever he wants done."

6. At the edge of the patio were six large empty stone pots that were used to purify water, each about the size of half a barrel,

7. Jesus said, "Okay, let's do it. Please fill all those water pots with fresh water." And so the helpers did as he asked, filling them all to the top.

8. And then Jesus said, "Now go get some wine jars and fill them from those pots and take them first to the guests at the head table and then serve the rest of the party."

9. When the helpers did as instructed, they suddenly realized what had just happened. What a moment before had been plain water, was now wine. So they took the jars of wine to the head table, where the people had no idea about what had just happened. After tasting the

¹⁰And saith unto him, Every man at the beginning doth set forth good wine; and when men have well drunk, then that which is worse: *but* thou hast kept the good wine until now.

¹¹This beginning of miracles did Jesus in Cana of Galilee, and manifested forth his glory; and his disciples believed on him.

¹²After this he went down to Capernaum, he, and his mother, and his brethren, and his disciples: and they continued there not many days.

¹³And the Jews' passover was at hand, and Jesus went up to Jerusalem,

¹⁴And found in the temple those that sold oxen and sheep and doves, and the changers of money sitting:

Chapter Two: Happiness Makes the Wedding Complete

wine, the man at the head of the table told the waiter to go get the bridegroom.

10. He told the bridegroom, "At feasts like this most folks will serve the best wine first. And then after everybody has drunk enough and can't really tell the difference, they bring out the cheap stuff. But I can taste what you've done, good fellow. You've saved the best for last!"

11. Of course, word spread among the helpers and from there to Jesus' new friends about how Jesus was apparently so happy, so at ease that things were happening around him that appeared miraculous. Jesus apparently had a handle on the underlying laws of the universe and practiced them so well that he could exhibit happiness and harmony where it seemed impossible. His new friends now recognized just how real, unique and special this wonderful new teacher was going to be.

12. After the wedding Jesus and his mother and his brothers and many of his new friends went and spent a couple of days at the seaside.

13. An old fashioned independence day was coming up, where the people of the tribe traditionally celebrated the escape of their great, great grandparents to a new land after years and years of forced, unpaid work under very harsh and violent bosses. Jesus agreed to go with the others to the city for the celebration.

14. The communal meeting hall in the city had originally been built as a quiet retreat for all the people to gather regardless of age, race, gender or social status. The hall was a place for all people to come together and be happy, to celebrate their freedom and the blessing of this new land. All the tribe was welcome. No one should have to pay to get in. But when Jesus arrived he found the meeting hall had been taken over by commercial vendors and bullies, and people had to pay for everything. Everybody was haggling over prices and exchange rates and what the price of admission to the hall would be.

[15] And when he had made a scourge of small cords, he drove them all out of the temple, and the sheep, and the oxen; and poured out the changers' money, and overthrew the tables;

[16] And said unto them that sold doves, Take these things hence; make not my Father's house an house of merchandise.

[17] And his disciples remembered that it was written, The zeal of thine house hath eaten me up.

[18] Then answered the Jews and said unto him, What sign shewest thou unto us, seeing that thou doest these things?

[19] Jesus answered and said unto them, Destroy this temple, and in three days I will raise it up.

[20] Then said the Jews, Forty and six years was this temple in building, and wilt thou rear it up in three days?

[21] But he spake of the temple of his body.

Chapter Two: Happiness Makes the Wedding Complete

15. Because Jesus was totally at peace with himself and others meant that he was also totally alive and free and brave and robust. "What the hell's going on in here?" he shouted, with a grin on his face He wasn't losing his cool. He was simply doing what he saw needed to be done in that moment. He grabbed a broom that had been laying up against the wall. "Okay, everybody out," he shouted as he started swinging it around, sweeping the vendors and ticket changers away from the entrance. "Move it! Move it!" he shouted. He knocked over the change boxes, and laughed. When the bullies saw this wild guy swinging a broom they quickly picked up their merchandise and left.

16. "This meeting hall is supposed to be a retreat where we can share our happiness, our peace," Jesus said. "Happiness doesn't depend on anything we can buy."

17. And Jesus' friends who were with him remembered that the scriptural traditions had warned against getting carried away with outer activities and trinkets which can so easily cover up our simple every day awareness, our innate happiness.

18. But the regulars there in the meeting hall weren't at all pleased with what Jesus was doing. "Who do you think you are," they asked, "to do these things here in our meeting house? Who gave you the authority to tell us how to run this place?"

19. "Happiness itself gives me authority," Jesus said. "Even if you tore down the whole outer structure of this hall, happiness would have it back up in three days' time. Happiness itself is indestructible."

20. "Yea, right," the people said. "Do you know how long it took us to build this place? Forty-six years! And you say happiness would have it back up in three days?"

21. Knowing in his heart what these folks were going to do to him in the not too distant future, Jesus was subtly

²²When therefore he was risen from the dead, his disciples remembered that he had said this unto them; and they believed the scripture, and the word which Jesus had said.

²³Now when he was in Jerusalem at the passover, in the feast *day*, many believed in his name, when they saw the miracles which he did.

²⁴But Jesus did not commit himself unto them, because he knew all *men*,

²⁵And needed not that any should testify of man: for he knew what was in man.

Chapter 3

¹There was a man of the Pharisees, named Nicodemus, a ruler of the Jews:

²The same came to Jesus by night, and said unto him, Rabbi, we know that thou art a teacher come from God: for no man can do these miracles that thou doest, except God be with him.

referring to the outer structure of his own body. But for the moment, he let it rest.

22. Later, when these folks did break down Jesus' body and sealed it into a mountain tomb, and then three days later Jesus walked back out of the tomb, his friends remembered his words here, about how he would raise it back up again. This helped them to know Jesus better and understand the indestructible power of happiness.

23. On that day in the city when all the people were relaxing together and eating and drinking, celebrating their independence, it was becoming more and more obvious to many people that Jesus' strong happiness was the cause of many healings and unexpected blessings.

24. Jesus rested as awareness itself. His center was happiness itself. He would politely refrain from making promises to anyone about doing this or that, even though they asked him to. He knew that most people, due to ignorance, inadvertently put limitations and conditions on awareness, which is another name for happiness.

25. Because Jesus had a clear sense of the unshakeable presence of perfect joy, he didn't need, and wasn't looking for fame or fortune or political position. He didn't need to play those games, so he didn't.

Chapter 3

1. One of the appointed governors in the area was a well-to-do local man named Nicodemus.

2. He came to Jesus one night after everybody had left and said, "We've been watching you. It's clear that there's something very special going on with you, and in you. The happiness that you radiate, and the healings and prospering that take place around you are obviously real, and must come from a very deep understanding of the

³Jesus answered and said unto him, Verily, verily, I say unto thee, Except a man be born again, he cannot see the kingdom of God.

⁴Nicodemus saith unto him, How can a man be born when he is old? can he enter the second time into his mother's womb, and be born?

⁵Jesus answered, Verily, verily, I say unto thee, Except a man be born of water and *of* the Spirit, he cannot enter into the kingdom of God.

⁶That which is born of the flesh is flesh; and that which is born of the Spirit is spirit.

⁷Marvel not that I said unto thee, Ye must be born again.

⁸The wind bloweth where it listeth, and thou hearest the sound thereof, but canst not tell whence it cometh, and whither it goeth: so is every one that is born of the Spirit.

Chapter Three: Awareness is Always Present

laws of the universe. You couldn't be doing what you are doing unless you were deeply connected with the underlying power, or force of reality. How do you do it?"

3. Jesus smiled and said, "In order to feel the joy, the peace that rules the world, inside and out, a person has to go beyond his acquired mental conditioning and again be with the simple awareness, the pure attention that he knew when he was first born, when he was a child."

4. Nicodemus asked, "How can a person who has accumulated all his worldly conditioning through all his life experience return to the attention, or awareness of a newborn? Of a child? Is it possible, or even desirable, to start all over again?"

5. Jesus answered, "Your awareness is always here, present, pure, clear, free, without any accumulated baggage. Return your attention to awareness itself, which is happiness itself, peace itself. Awareness itself is eternal, timeless, space-less, undying. Awareness itself, without all the accumulated baggage, is infinite love, living joy.

6. "Temporary things rise and fall in awareness—including the physical body and daily concerns and thoughts and feelings. But awareness itself does not come and go. Until you begin paying attention to awareness itself, you can't help but be caught up with all the temporary risings and fallings, and you're unable to rest in your true nature.

7. "Don't be so surprised that I encourage you to return to your original nature, to the pure awareness you knew as a child. It's really not such a hard thing to do.

8. "When you are resting in awareness itself things rise and fall, come and go, but you as awareness are not unduly worried, not moved by the ongoing ruckus. The images and events that rise up in awareness are like the wind: you

⁹Nicodemus answered and said unto him, How can these things be?

¹⁰Jesus answered and said unto him, Art thou a master of Israel, and knowest not these things?

¹¹Verily, verily, I say unto thee, We speak that we do know, and testify that we have seen; and ye receive not our witness.

¹²If I have told you earthly things, and ye believe not, how shall ye believe, if I tell you *of* heavenly things?

¹³And no man hath ascended up to heaven, but he that came down from heaven, *even* the Son of man which is in heaven.

¹⁴And as Moses lifted up the serpent in the wilderness, even so must the Son of man be lifted up

¹⁵That whosoever believeth in him should not perish, but have eternal life.

Chapter Three: Awareness is Always Present

can't really tell where they came from, or where they are going, but your presence here—your awareness, your happiness —is unmoved by the wind that continually rises and falls, comes and goes."

9. Nicodemus was struck by Jesus' words. He asked, "Can our return to happiness really be this simple, this direct?"

10. Jesus smiled. He said, "Nicodemus, you're one of the leaders, a governor of our whole area. Isn't this the type of simple and direct guidance toward their own natural happiness that the people want from their leaders?

11. "I'm simply sharing my own direct experience of these things, of happiness and awareness. I'm not philosophizing or making these things up. I encourage you to take the time to observe your own inner processes to verify whether these observations are accurate.

12. "I'm pointing to something very close at hand—the presence of your own inner joy, which is the nature of your daily awareness. If you don't yet grasp the power of these very simple and ordinary things, how will you understand or grasp the wider, deeper powers into which these simple things will lead you?

13. "No one ever arrives at true joy, or deep peace, until they finally understand that this is also their starting place. Happiness or peace, is the essence of every human being.

14. "All of the scriptures in every culture have pointed to this basic fact. It is this native inner joy that has lifted and evolved human beings up from their un-evolved beginnings. It is this joy that is at work in me and lifts and animates me.

15. "This same joy will lift and animate and empower anyone who understands its presence and turns inward to

[16] For God so loved the world, that he gave his only begotten Son, that whosoever believeth in him should not perish, but have everlasting life.

[17] For God sent not his Son into the world to condemn the world; but that the world through him might be saved.

[18] He that believeth on him is not condemned: but he that believeth not is condemned already, because he hath not believed in the name of the only begotten Son of God.

[19] And this is the condemnation, that light is come into the world, and men loved darkness rather than light, because their deeds were evil.

Chapter Three: Awareness is Always Present

access it. This inner light is the undying presence, the eternal light that guides us even after we have dropped the body.

16. "Awareness, or joy is the sustainer and animator of the planet and everything on it, and of the solar system and of the entire universe. This same joy is present in each of us. When we recognize joy's infinite, ever-present quality, and allow it to be our guide and our motivator, we harmonize with the universe itself, and spontaneously blossom into our original, native, natural radiance.

17. "I've been practicing joy, resting in awareness. I allow it to be my very life. You can learn from my example. Our joy is what enlivens us. It is what saves us from all the woes and worries and unnecessary suffering, physical, mental and emotional, that we bring upon ourselves when we don't recognize the purpose of life, which is simply to love, to enjoy, to be happy.

18. "For the people who recognize that awareness, or joy is their essence, and that this happiness is always available, their lives seem to continually blossom and are full of grace and ease. Things consistently work out well for them. But for the people who do not recognize their natural happiness, and who do not consciously cultivate joy in their lives by putting their attention on it, their daily consciousness becomes heavy and dark. It is because of this heavy consciousness that their problems seems to grow, one problem piled on the next problem. Somehow they never seem to get out from under their troubles.

19. "It's sad that people have not learned this simple truth that what we put our attention on, grows. Our natural happiness is already here, already present, but people ignore it, skip over it, refuse to acknowledge it. Happiness is here for everybody but a large number of people fix their attention not on happiness but rather on their problems, their troubles, their sufferings. Their attention is

²⁰For every one that doeth evil hateth the light, neither cometh to the light, lest his deeds should be reproved.

²¹But he that doeth truth cometh to the light, that his deeds may be made manifest, that they are wrought in God.

²²After these things came Jesus and his disciples into the land of Judaea; and there he tarried with them, and baptized.

²³And John also was baptizing in Aenon near to Salim, because there was much water there: and they came, and were baptized.

²⁴For John was not yet cast into prison.

²⁵Then there arose a question between *some* of John's disciples and the Jews about purifying.

²⁶And they came unto John, and said unto him, Rabbi, he that was with thee beyond Jordan, to whom thou barest witness, behold, the same baptizeth, and all *men* come to him.

locked on unhappiness, and thus unhappiness grows. And this is what they identify with.

20. "Curiously, when people are identified with their own unhappiness, happiness itself appears to them as a foreign intruder, a lie, a threat, not to be trusted. So they shrink away from happiness, guarding and protecting their unhappiness.

21. "But, thankfully, more and more folks are beginning to recognize the reality of happiness, and have begun to put their attention on it. More and more people are beginning to practice happiness every day, allowing it to flow in and through and around everything they think and say and do. These people are a blessing, to themselves, and to their families and to the whole world."

22. These are some of the things that Jesus taught. He and his friends went to the country and stayed together, and his very presence was a blessing to them and to all the people who came to see him and be with him. He was introducing all of them to their own native joy.

3.John the Baptist was also teaching happiness, in his own way, in an area nearby where many people were very open to the process.

24. John had not yet encountered his troubles or been put in jail for teaching happiness, like he would be later on.

25. A question came up among some of John's friends and the people he was teaching about the best way to practice and intensify happiness.

26. So they went to John and said, "Okay, tell us. That fellow that was with you the other day, that you said was happiness itself, he's also teaching and showing the way of happiness. Many people are flocking to him. Is that good?"

²⁷John answered and said, A man can receive nothing, except it be given him from heaven.

²⁸Ye yourselves bear me witness, that I said, I am not the Christ, but that I am sent before him.

²⁹He that hath the bride is the bridegroom: but the friend of the bridegroom, which standeth and heareth him, rejoiceth greatly because of the bridegroom's voice: this my joy therefore is fulfilled.

³⁰He must increase, but I *must* decrease.

³¹He that cometh from above is above all: he that is of the earth is earthly, and speaketh of the earth: he that cometh from heaven is above all.

³²And what he hath seen and heard, that he testifieth; and no man receiveth his testimony.

³³He that hath received his testimony hath set to his seal that God is true.

27. John said "Yes, every circumstance arises out of happiness itself. Anything and everything that comes to us that is real and true comes from happiness.

28. "I've already told you that I myself have not yet learned how to always identify with awareness, with happiness, and yet I know it is possible. It is that basic identification with happiness itself that I've been encouraging.

29. "And now we have a man here with us who is totally married to happiness. It's as if he's the groom and his bride is happiness. I'm like the best man. I stand up with him. And because he's doing what he's doing, showing us the way, I am totally happy to be here with him. Because of him, I understand and experience my own happiness much more directly, much more completely.

30. "In his presence, in the presence of awareness itself, happiness itself, I more easily, more spontaneously let go of my false identities. Because of him my natural happiness, my awareness becomes ever more apparent.

31. "Awareness, joy, love, is what life is all about. We get so caught up in all our daily intentions and machinations that we forget about what is real. Like almost everybody else I myself tend to get caught up in all of life's daily problems and sometimes can't see the forest for the trees. But when a person has dropped, or at least seen through, all false, limited identities and returned to the first identity, which is awareness itself, happiness itself, then that person's life becomes clear and simple and true.

32. "I'm sharing with you only that which I have experienced in my own life. Our culture and training keeps most people from recognizing these simple truths about love, joy and awareness.

33. "Nevertheless, if you explore your own inner depths and see the joy there, the peace that is life itself—if you just

[34] For he whom God hath sent speaketh the words of God: for God giveth not the Spirit by measure *unto him*.

[35] The Father loveth the Son, and hath given all things into his hand.

[36] He that believeth on the Son hath everlasting life: and he that believeth not the Son shall not see life; but the wrath of God abideth on him.

Chapter Four

[1] When therefore the Lord knew how the Pharisees had heard that Jesus made and baptized more disciples than John,

[2] (Though Jesus himself baptized not, but his disciples,)

recognize that your own daily awareness is joy itself, life itself --- you will then know that what I have been sharing with you is real. Once you recognize that the joy within you is the same as the joy outside of you, the life within you is the life of the universe, you will never be able to forget such an observation.

34. "You will discover that even though it appears as though it is me, John, speaking to you in this way, it is in fact your own inner life that is speaking to you from without. Nothing is impossible for joy, or too good.

35. "Happiness, or awareness, expresses itself in an infinite variety of ways, in eternal artistry. We are each expressions of the same life. As we turn to joy, rest in joy, our expressions grow, radiate and flourish in the world.

36. "When we turn our attention again and again to joy, to love, to awareness, we are remembering life itself, the eternal presence in which all forms rise and fall. When our attention gets entangled in all the forms and dramas and speculations that continually arise in our lives, and we ignore happiness or make it into some far off reward, our lives are diminished, made less than they might be because the very juice of life has been denied. When we deny, or forget the happiness that is behind all form and dramas, we are at the mercy of the forms and the dramas."

Chapter Four

1. The word quickly spread that Jesus' very presence was happiness itself. Jesus was aware that the word was spreading and that those who promised the reward of happiness through other rites and rituals would not necessarily welcome his presence.

2. (Jesus himself didn't need to spread the word. He was simply present, as himself. It was his close friends who spread the word and brought all manner of people to him.)

³He left Judaea, and departed again into Galilee.

⁴And he must needs go through Samaria.

⁵Then cometh he to a city of Samaria, which is called Sychar, near to the parcel of ground that Jacob gave to his son Joseph.

⁶Now Jacob's well was there. Jesus therefore, being wearied with *his* journey, sat thus on the well: *and* it was about the sixth hour.

⁷There cometh a woman of Samaria to draw water: Jesus saith unto her, Give me to drink.

⁸(For his disciples were gone away unto the city to buy meat.)

⁹Then saith the woman of Samaria unto him, How is it that thou, being a Jew, askest drink of me, which am a woman of Samaria? for the Jews have no dealings with the Samaritans.

¹⁰Jesus answered and said unto her, If thou knewest the gift of God, and who it is that saith to thee, Give me to drink; thou wouldest have asked of him, and he would have given thee living water.

¹¹The woman saith unto him, Sir, thou hast nothing to draw with, and the well is deep: from whence then hast thou that living water?

Chapter Four: The Well of Joy Never Runs Dry

3. To do his work, and keep a low profile, Jesus kept moving, traveling from one place to another.

4. While on his travels, he came to one of the more popular mountain towns.

5. It was an old town, with much history and folklore. Many famous people had lived there in the past and many different tribes who didn't always get along.

6. There was an old well in the center of town. It was late and it had been a long day of traveling so Jesus took a seat near the well.

7. One of the women of the town came by to draw some water out of the well. Jesus said, "Pardon me, but would you mind also getting me a drink?"

8. (Ordinarily, one of Jesus' friends would have already made sure he had something to drink, as they were all very happy to serve him in whatever way they could. But at the time all of his friends had gone off to the market to get the makings for dinner.)

9. The lady was surprised. She said, "I thought people from your tribe didn't talk to people from my tribe. You people say we aren't good enough for you. You folks generally don't even acknowledge our presence. So why are you willing to have me get you a drink of water?"

10. Jesus grinned. "Friend," he said, "if you knew your own happiness, and could see who it was that was asking you for a simple drink, you might have as easily asked me for a drink, to quench your thirst with my own waters. I would be more than willing to do so. And then you would never be thirsty again."

11. "What are you talking about?" the woman asked. "You don't even have a bucket or a jar to get the water out of the

¹²Art thou greater than our father Jacob, which gave us the well, and drank thereof himself, and his children, and his cattle?
¹³·Jesus answered and said unto her, Whosoever drinketh of this water shall thirst again:

¹⁴But whosoever drinketh of the water that I shall give him shall never thirst; but the water that I shall give him shall be in him a well of water springing up into everlasting life.

¹⁵The woman saith unto him, Sir, give me this water, that I thirst not, neither come hither to draw.

¹⁶Jesus saith unto her, Go, call thy husband, and come hither.

¹⁷The woman answered and said, I have no husband. Jesus said unto her, Thou hast well said, I have no husband:

¹⁸For thou hast had five husbands; and he whom thou now hast is not thy husband: in that saidst thou truly.

¹⁹The woman saith unto him, Sir, I perceive that thou art a prophet.

Chapter Four: The Well of Joy Never Runs Dry

the well. And that well is very deep. So how would you get me any of this magical water you're talking about?

12. "Besides, this is a very famous well. People have been coming here for as long as anybody can remember, and it's been giving us all the water we need, not only for ourselves but for our livestock. And now you tell me you have better water than this?"

13. "What you say is true," Jesus said. "But you have to keep coming back to this well. The water you get here only quenches your thirst for a little while.

14. "What I'm pointing to is the wellspring of happiness that never runs dry that is inside you and inside me and inside everybody. When we start to draw from that well, we never get thirsty, because our lives are spontaneously nourished by an eternal presence that is always available."

15. The woman was moved by his words. "Okay," she said. "Show me how to get the water that quenches my thirst for good, so that I don't ever have to come to the well again."

16. Again Jesus smiled. "Sure," he said. "First, go get your husband. Bring him here. We'll all talk."

17. The woman was a bit embarrassed. "I don't have a husband," she said. Jesus nodded. "I know," he said.

18. "And I also know that up until now you have had five husbands, and the fellow you are now living with is not your husband. So you were telling the truth when you said you have no husband."

19. The woman looked at him and didn't say anything for a moment. And then she said, "You see things, don't you? You can see things that most people don't see, like through time and space.

²⁰Our fathers worshipped in this mountain; and ye say, that in Jerusalem is the place where men ought to worship.

²¹Jesus saith unto her, Woman, believe me, the hour cometh, when ye shall neither in this mountain, nor yet at Jerusalem, worship the Father.

²²Ye worship ye know not what: we know what we worship: for salvation is of the Jews.

²³But the hour cometh, and now is, when the true worshippers shall worship the Father in spirit and in truth: for the Father seeketh such to worship him.

²⁴God *is* a Spirit: and they that worship him must worship *him* in spirit and in truth.

²⁵The woman saith unto him, I know that Messias cometh, which is called Christ: when he is come, he will tell us all things.

²⁶Jesus saith unto her, I that speak unto thee am *he*.

²⁷And upon this came his disciples, and marvelled that he talked with the woman: yet no man said, What seekest thou? or, Why talkest thou with her?

Chapter Four: The Well of Joy Never Runs Dry

[20.] "So tell me. People from my tribe have been struggling to find happiness here in these mountains for a long time but people from your tribe insist that the only place to find happiness is in your big temple in the city. Is that true?"

[21.] Jesus said, "No. Happiness is not a matter of place. It's always in the moment, wherever you are.

[22.] "Most people assume happiness, which is the fullness of life, is something far away, something foreign and fleeting. I'm here to point out that happiness, which is your awareness, your wholeness, is always close at hand.

[23.] "Happiness is our true nature. It is natural and right that we enjoy our happiness wherever we are. Happiness is the living water, it is life itself, it is what life is all about. We have all come to earth to learn and practice the happiness art.

[24.] "Happiness itself is formless, timeless, space-less. It does not require form or time or space, and yet it is very simple and free and everybody knows exactly what it is. We discover our natural selves in happiness, which is awareness itself, whether we are in the mountains or the city. We can allow attention to rest in awareness time and again. This is as our rightful and natural daily discipline."

[25.] The woman said, "I've heard that happiness will some day take on a human form and that when happiness takes on its human form then that human will teach us all how to understand and embody happiness, in our own being."

[26.] Jesus smiled and nodded. "Yes, what you say is true," he said. "And I am that human form of happiness itself."

[27.] At this point Jesus' friends returned from the market and were somewhat surprised to find Jesus and the woman talking so deeply, so happily together. But nobody

²⁸The woman then left her waterpot, and went her way into the city, and saith to the men,

²⁹Come, see a man, which told me all things that ever I did: is not this the Christ?

³⁰Then they went out of the city, and came unto him.

³¹In the mean while his disciples prayed him, saying, Master, eat.

³²But he said unto them, I have meat to eat that ye know not of.

³³Therefore said the disciples one to another, Hath any man brought him *ought* to eat?

³⁴Jesus saith unto them, My meat is to do the will of him that sent me, and to finish his work.

³⁵Say not ye, There are yet four months, and *then* cometh harvest? behold, I say unto you, Lift up your eyes, and look on the fields; for they are white already to harvest.

Chapter Four: The Well of Joy Never Runs Dry

said anything either to Jesus or the woman about what was going on between them.

28. The woman had been very moved by Jesus' words, and his very presence. She left her water jugs there at the well and she herself went to town to tell her neighbors.

29. "You have to come meet this fellow I just talked to," she said to the people in town. "First off, he knew all about my own personal history without even asking. And he explains everything very simply, very clearly, in a very helpful way. There is something very real and lovely and beautiful about this man."

30. So quite a few people from the town went out to where Jesus and his friends were staying.

31. Meanwhile, Jesus' friends had fixed some of the food they had picked up in town and were encouraging him to sit down and eat.

32. Jesus smiled and said, "I'm already full. I'm always full. I'm always being fed and nourished because food is coming to me all the time. You're just not seeing it."

33. Jesus' friends looked at each other inquisitively. "Has anybody brought him something to eat?" they asked. "Maybe somebody we don't know about?"

34. Again Jesus explained. "I am nourished by happiness itself. Sustained by awareness itself. That's what I am. Fed by happiness I never go hungry. I am always complete, always satisfied, and those around me are likewise complete and satisfied.

35. "Harvest time is always right now, here, today. Our happiness does not depend on putting seeds in the ground, watering, weeding, and hoping for good weather

³⁶And he that reapeth receiveth wages, and gathereth fruit unto life eternal: that both he that soweth and he that reapeth may rejoice together.

³⁷And herein is that saying true, One soweth, and another reapeth.

³⁸I sent you to reap that whereon ye bestowed no labour: other men laboured, and ye are entered into their labours.

³⁹And many of the Samaritans of that city believed on him for the saying of the woman, which testified, He told me all that ever I did.

⁴⁰So when the Samaritans were come unto him, they besought him that he would tarry with them: and he abode there two days.

⁴¹And many more believed because of his own word;

Chapter Four: The Well of Joy Never Runs Dry

and fortunate circumstances before we reap. Happiness is always already full, complete, within and without, available to feed and nourish us, right here, right now.

36. "When we turn our attention to happiness itself, which resides as awareness itself, we begin to free ourselves of the bonds of time and space. Awareness opens the doors to everything and everyone that has gone before and everything and everyone that will come after.

37. "We are all in it together. One person's seed of happiness becomes another person's blossom of happiness. One person's blossom is the next person's seed. The happiness is the same. The awareness doesn't change. It is that which brings the seed to blossom and the blossom to seed.

38. "Our own understanding of happiness here now is possible because of the understanding of happiness that others before us have gathered. And what we do with happiness now will likewise feed others in their own time. Like I said. We're in it together. Happiness is for everybody, since it is the essence of awareness."

39. Many of the people from the town believed him and understood him—including the idea that happiness empowers one to even transcend time and space-- because he had proven the truth of his words when he told the woman at the well about her previous husbands and the fact that the man she was now with was not her husband.

40. Jesus was suddenly very popular among these people. They wanted him to stick around and teach them more. So for the next two days he stayed with them and taught them and generally showed them how to be happy for no reason in particular.

41. The longer he stayed with them, the more they understood and brought others of the town to come and also partake.

⁴²And said unto the woman, Now we believe, not because of thy saying: for we have heard *him* ourselves, and know that this is indeed the Christ, the Saviour of the world.

⁴³Now after two days he departed thence, and went into Galilee.

⁴⁴For Jesus himself testified, that a prophet hath no honour in his own country.

⁴⁵Then when he was come into Galilee, the Galilaeans received him, having seen all the things that he did at Jerusalem at the feast: for they also went unto the feast.

⁴⁶So Jesus came again into Cana of Galilee, where he made the water wine. And there was a certain nobleman, whose son was sick at Capernaum.

⁴⁷When he heard that Jesus was come out of Judaea into Galilee, he went unto him, and besought him that he would come down, and heal his son: for he was at the point of death.

⁴⁸Then said Jesus unto him, Except ye see signs and wonders, ye will not believe.

Chapter Four: The Well of Joy Never Runs Dry

⁴². The townspeople then assured the woman from the well that they themselves had now experienced what she had experienced, and that yes, this man truly was happiness itself. Jesus had demonstrated for them the beauty and power and simplicity of happiness itself, and what it meant to be fully identified with that essence, that joyful presence that never dies.

⁴³·After several days with these folks Jesus and his friends continued on their journey, moving even further from the area where Jesus had been brought up.

⁴⁴· Jesus had observed that when something special, beautiful and true is unfolding in somebody that the people who are most familiar with that person are generally the last to recognize it.

⁴⁵. In the next province Jesus and his friends were warmly welcomed and taken care of because Jesus' reputation had preceded him. Many of the people in this area had also been guests at the recent marriage in that city where Jesus first demonstrated the power of happiness. Many here had drank the fine wine that his happiness had inspired.

⁴⁶· Soon he was back again in the exact village where the new wine had been served, among many people who knew what his happiness might inspire. One of the rich men of the village, who was also a councilman, had a son who was quite ill in another village some distance away.

⁴⁷· When this man heard that Jesus had returned and was there in the village, he went to him right away and asked him, pleaded with him to go to the distant village to help his son. His son was near death, he said, and truly needed a miracle.

⁴⁸· "Perfect joy, which is life's essence, is always present within us," Jesus said. "Most people overlook this inner harmony unless and until they have some outer proof, or

⁴⁹The nobleman saith unto him, Sir, come down ere my child die.

⁵⁰Jesus saith unto him, Go thy way; thy son liveth. And the man believed the word that Jesus had spoken unto him, and he went his way.

⁵¹And as he was now going down, his servants met him, and told *him*, saying, Thy son liveth.

⁵²Then enquired he of them the hour when he began to amend. And they said unto him, Yesterday at the seventh hour the fever left him.

⁵³So the father knew that *it was* at the same hour, in the which Jesus said unto him, Thy son liveth: and himself believed, and his whole house.

⁵⁴This *is* again the second miracle *that* Jesus did, when he was come out of Judaea into Galilee.

Chapter 5

¹After this there was a feast of the Jews; and Jesus went up to Jerusalem.

some outer demonstration of the inner harmony. Yet life's wholeness is always everywhere present."

[49] "Please," the man begged, ignoring Jesus' observation, "Please, come help me. My son is near death."

[50]. "You go ahead," Jesus said. "I don't need to be there in person. Trust me, your son will be okay. He'll recover fully." Because of the way Jesus said these things, the man believed him. He was very relieved and headed off to see his son in a town which was several days journey away.

[51] The next day, as he was still on his way, some of his household staff met him and told him the good news that his son had suddenly recovered, the crisis had passed and his son was now up and about.

[52] The man asked his staff what time his son had begun to recover. They told him that it had been yesterday morning that the son's fever had suddenly broke and then began to recover.

[53]. It was obvious to the father that this was the same time that he had spoken with Jesus, and Jesus had told him things would be okay. It was the same hour when he had felt a relief, and a certainty in Jesus words.

[54]. So again, Jesus demonstrated the power and grace that unfolds when one is identified with happiness itself. Just as he did when turning water into wine, he showed with this healing that deep harmony can be expected, and is the first law of human experience.

Chapter 5.

[1] In the big city another gathering of the tribe for a major traditional celebration was being held. Again, Jesus and his friends decided to go.

²Now there is at Jerusalem by the sheep *market* a pool, which is called in the Hebrew tongue Bethesda, having five porches.

³In these lay a great multitude of impotent folk, of blind, halt, withered, waiting for the moving of the water.

⁴For an angel went down at a certain season into the pool, and troubled the water: whosoever then first after the troubling of the water stepped in was made whole of whatsoever disease he had.

⁵And a certain man was there, which had an infirmity thirty and eight years.

⁶When Jesus saw him lie, and knew that he had been now a long time *in that case*, he saith unto him, Wilt thou be made whole?

⁷The impotent man answered him, Sir, I have no man, when the water is troubled, to put me into the pool: but while I am coming, another steppeth down before me.

⁸Jesus saith unto him, Rise, take up thy bed, and walk.

⁹And immediately the man was made whole, and took up his bed, and walked: and on the same day was the sabbath.

Chapter five: Happiness is Undying

2. In that city by the market was a large pool surrounded by nice porches. The locals referred to this place as the house of mercy.

3. The reason they called it this is because this is where people with many types of physical and mental problems came and waited, hoping for a miracle to take place, which sometimes actually happened when the water in the pool became ruffled. Because of the history of miracles, blind and crippled people and many others with other problems all gathered and waited around the pool.

4. The story among the people was that some invisible, joyful healing spirit would occasionally visit the pool. Although this spirit was invisible you could tell it had been there because the waters became ruffled. Folks believed that whoever could first get into the water after the joyful spirit had ruffled the waters might get a healing.

5. One poor fellow who had been crippled and suffering for almost forty years was laying on an old mattress there by the pool. He had lain there most of his life. He couldn't walk or even stand, that's why he had his mattress.

6. Jesus saw the fellow, and being able to see through time and space Jesus knew the poor fellow's history. "Friend," Jesus said, "are you willing to reconnect with the joy that will make you whole again?"

7. The fellow said, "Yes, of course, but I can't. I don't have anybody to lift me up and put me in the pool after the spirit of joy ruffles the waters. I try to make it to the pool by myself, but somebody always gets there before me."

8. Jesus said, "That pool is already within you. You've been in it all along. You can stand up and walk right now."

9. Just the way Jesus said it, with love, confidence and understanding, the fellow recognized it was true. He

¹⁰The Jews therefore said unto him that was cured, It is the sabbath day: it is not lawful for thee to carry *thy* bed.

¹¹He answered them, He that made me whole, the same said unto me, Take up thy bed, and walk.

¹²Then asked they him, What man is that which said unto thee, Take up thy bed, and walk?

¹³And he that was healed wist not who it was: for Jesus had conveyed himself away, a multitude being in *that* place.

¹⁴Afterward Jesus findeth him in the temple, and said unto him, Behold, thou art made whole: sin no more, lest a worse thing come unto thee.

¹⁵The man departed, and told the Jews that it was Jesus, which had made him whole.

¹⁶And therefore did the Jews persecute Jesus, and sought to slay him, because he had done these things on the sabbath day.

suddenly felt the living joy inside him, felt the happiness that was his true nature. This was the same joy that Jesus himself had learned to identify with completely. The fellow grinned, then laughed, suddenly felt completely whole. He stood up, shook himself, laughed again. He was feeling so good he even reached down and lifted up his mattress. He did a little jig. It was supposed to be a holy day, there in the city, when people were forbidden to do any work, or lifting of any kind. The fellow didn't care.

10. The elders there in the tribe, watching him, reminded him that it was a holy day and no one was supposed to do lifting work. They told him he shouldn't be carrying his old mattress.

11. The fellow said to them, "Hey, the man who showed me my wholeness, who connected me again with the life force, told me I could stand up, walk, and carry this old thing."

12. The elders of his tribe asked him, "Who was it that said that? Who showed you how to do this?"

13. The guy looked around but there was a big crowd coming and going. Jesus had easily slipped away into the crowd, and the fellow didn't know who he was.

14. But later on at the meeting house Jesus ran into the same fellow. "Stick with your joy," Jesus reminded him. "Keep your loyalty to your inner happiness. If you don't, then out of old habit you'll start to focus on outer unhappiness again, and then you'll draw all sorts of new miseries your way. So stick with your joy. Honor it always."

15. The man thanked him, and then left and went and told the leaders of the tribe that it was that nice fellow Jesus who had showed him how to be healthy again.

16. So the leaders of the tribe had more evidence against Jesus, for working on a holy day and encouraging others to

[17] But Jesus answered them, My Father worketh hitherto, and I work.

[18] Therefore the Jews sought the more to kill him, because he not only had broken the sabbath, but said also that God was his Father, making himself equal with God.

[19] Then answered Jesus and said unto them, Verily, verily, I say unto you, The Son can do nothing of himself, but what he seeth the Father do: for what things soever he doeth, these also doeth the Son likewise.

[20] For the Father loveth the Son, and sheweth him all things that himself doeth: and he will shew him greater works than these, that ye may marvel.

[21] For as the Father raiseth up the dead, and quickeneth *them*; even so the Son quickeneth whom he will

do likewise. They started to plot secretly on how to put a stop to him, and even do away with him, if they could. They would soon confront him with all their evidence.

17. Jesus wasn't worried. "It's joy, it's awareness itself that is working in me and through me," he said. "The joy that is in me is the same joy that created the universe. Are these men going to put a stop to the universe itself?"

18. These words made the elders even more suspicious, and even more determined to do away with Jesus. They assumed that working on the holy day was a crime in itself. But they felt it was outright blasphemy for Jesus to suggest that the power that was working in him and through him was the power of the whole universe.

19. Jesus stood his ground. "It's true," he said. "The happiness that moves the universe moves me. I can't do anything without that power. When the universal joy moves, I have no option: I, too, must move. I and joy move as one. I and life move as one.

20. "And that's not a bad thing. Happiness opens our inner doors and reveals the nature of the universe, past, present and future. Happiness brings out the harmony that had not been obvious. Happiness reveals what to ordinary senses seems miraculous. I've been taught to practice happiness, identify with happiness. Indeed, I was born to practice and identify with happiness. Every human being was born for the exact same purpose. What you've seen so far is just the beginning. Much more seemingly miraculous expressions of joy, of harmony are yet to be unfolded.

21. "Happiness is undying. What to our eyes appears as death, happiness shows to be a mirage. We've all known people who everybody thought was dead but have come back to life. When you identify with happiness, this is no longer a strange or unexplainable phenomenon. Identified with happiness I bring life to those around me, in

[22] For the Father judgeth no man, but hath committed all judgment unto the Son:

[23] That all *men* should honour the Son, even as they honour the Father. He that honoureth not the Son honoureth not the Father which hath sent him.

[24] Verily, verily, I say unto you, He that heareth my word, and believeth on him that sent me, hath everlasting life, and shall not come into condemnation; but is passed from death unto life.

[25] Verily, verily, I say unto you, The hour is coming, and now is, when the dead shall hear the voice of the Son of God: and they that hear shall live.

absolutely every way. Anybody who identifies with happiness will experience the same thing.

22. "The first and most fundamental question we can ask of ourselves is whether or not in this moment we are attending to happiness, within and without. Happiness is love. Happiness is life. If we aren't attending to happiness, we are attending to death.

23. "If we are attending to happiness, even in its simplest, most ordinary expressions, in ourselves and others, then we are aligning ourselves with life, with the universal presence. If we ignore happiness, downplay happiness, which is love itself, and insist on some other criteria for judging ourselves and others, then we are misguided, misjudging, and are thereby diminishing our own lives and the lives of those around us.

24. "What I am teaching here is very simple, very direct. If you simply attend more and more to basic awareness, which is your joy, your love, allowing it to be the most important force in your life, your life blossoms, grows, is of service to the whole planet. When you attend to awareness you attend to that life in you that never dies. You discover your life growing and blossoming and enriched in every possible way. Even the death of the body itself is no longer a worry or problem for you, because you are no longer identified with the body but rather with that which does not die.

25. "When I remind you in this way of the simple facts of being—that awareness is your first and lasting identity—such a reminder is an awakening; what you remember lifts you from your sleep, your lethargy, your trance. This remembrance, this call to awakening is not confined to those who still have their flesh body. Awareness knows no death, and no time. It is the eternal presence. So those who have gone before, and those who are yet to come, all can hear this call to remember their own life, their own

[26] For as the Father hath life in himself; so hath he given to the Son to have life in himself;

[27] And hath given him authority to execute judgment also, because he is the Son of man.

[28] Marvel not at this: for the hour is coming, in the which all that are in the graves shall hear his voice,

[29] And shall come forth; they that have done good, unto the resurrection of life; and they that have done evil, unto the resurrection of damnation.

happiness, or awareness. All who hear the call, and remember the simple presence of joy, awaken to more aliveness.

26. "Happiness, awareness and love are three words for the exact same living presence. This presence is at the root of the universe itself, is its substance. Thus, there is nothing in the universe that is not, at root, derived from and dependent upon happiness, or awareness. So we as human beings also have this happiness, this awareness at our core.

27. "Turning to this awareness, identified with this awareness, we are spontaneously at ease with ourselves, our neighbors, and life itself. We are whole, complete. Knowing such natural ease, we spontaneously support and guide and direct our own energies and the energies of those around us, including those who came to the flesh before us and those who will come to the flesh later.

28. "Having flesh—a body—or not having a body is not a barrier to this message of joy. Joy is here, available to every being, whether on this side or the other side of the veil. All people everywhere are now awakening to the simple truth of the undying presence of love, of happiness.

29. "As we recognize the joy within us, and put our attention on it, and allow it to be our first interest, our primary work, our daily companion, our first identity, then we quickly discover our lives unfolding with ever deeper grace, beauty and service. However, there are some folks who are so habituated to their own *unhappiness* that they have actually identified with it. To those who are identified with unhappiness, this call to remember happiness appears threatening, unbalancing, even blasphemous. Those who have mistakenly identified with unhappiness will therefore argue against this teaching, and refuse to practice it in their lives. They will stay stuck, at least for a while, in their misery.

³⁰I can of mine own self do nothing: as I hear, I judge: and my judgment is just; because I seek not mine own will, but the will of the Father which hath sent me.

³¹If I bear witness of myself, my witness is not true.

³²There is another that beareth witness of me; and I know that the witness which he witnesseth of me is true.

³³Ye sent unto John, and he bare witness unto the truth.

³⁴But I receive not testimony from man: but these things I say, that ye might be saved.

³⁵He was a burning and a shining light: and ye were willing for a season to rejoice in his light.

Chapter five: Happiness is Undying

30. "Happiness, which is the intelligent life force, moves through each of us. We on our own don't have a lot of say in the matter, even though we sometimes assume that we do. When we recognize that happiness rules, that joy, love, rules, our lives become much simpler. We can then, moment by moment, let happiness have its way, have its say in us and through us. When we let happiness take the lead, we always find ourselves in the right place at the right time, with the right people, saying and doing the right things. But we tend to outline happiness, put conditions on it, try to make it happen one way or another, appear in one form or another, according to personal will.

31. "But none of us has any reality, any life outside of awareness itself, outside of joy, or love. If we tried to stand outside of awareness, and then discuss it, where would we stand? Such a discussion is not possible.

32. "As friends, though, we can come together and discuss these things, recognize awareness, which is happiness, in our own lives and in the lives of those around us. When one of us points out the truth of these things, others recognize it in their own lives and confirm its validity.

33. "My friend John, for example, has been pointing to these same things, and when he and I met there was a recognition that happiness itself was present and flowing. He pointed out this happiness to you.

34. "Nevertheless, confirmation of our happiness does not come from the outside, but rather from within. We talk of these things, and receive these teachings from outside ourselves, but only so that we might confirm what is going on within ourselves.

35. "When John talked of happiness, of awareness, it was a new teaching for you. You were uplifted by his words, because his words pointed you to your own true nature.

³⁶But I have greater witness than *that* of John: for the works which the Father hath given me to finish, the same works that I do, bear witness of me, that the Father hath sent me.

³⁷And the Father himself, which hath sent me, hath borne witness of me. Ye have neither heard his voice at any time, nor seen his shape.

³⁸And ye have not his word abiding in you: for whom he hath sent, him ye believe not.

³⁹Search the scriptures; for in them ye think ye have eternal life: and they are they which testify of me.

⁴⁰And ye will not come to me, that ye might have life.

36. "I appreciate John's confident testimony, that he could recognize happiness fully alive and working in me, and through me. And yet John's word was only the beginning. As you will remember, the happiness working through me has brought about many healings for many people; the happiness has caused many wonderful unfoldings, and you have seen a great number of harmonious occurrences happening in my presence. All of these are in themselves the proof that happiness does indeed work in me, and through me, and that the teachings I am sharing with you are in fact teachings directly from happiness itself.

37. "The happy events that you have experienced in my presence are the proof that happiness is the source of my teaching. And yet, these outer proofs, the changing sounds and shapes and forms that are the result of happiness, are not happiness itself. Happiness itself, being undying, has no final form, or shape or sound. So many of you tend to doubt these teachings.

38. "I point to the happiness already alive there inside you but you still go looking for it elsewhere. I've shown you what good things happen in your life when you identify with your inner awareness, but many of you still want to make the experience of heaven on earth more complicated than this, still far off, not a part of your daily experience.

39. "What I am saying and teaching is not really new, is not out of the ordinary. If you will examine the scriptures of every culture you will discover that what I am sharing with you --- that your happiness, which is eternal and undying, is already here, complete and full within you--- is exactly what these scriptures have been teaching and pointing to for generations.

40. "Your lives could have no meaning, no power, no beauty without awareness. But obviously, your awareness is in fact here. I am here, teaching this way, and healing

⁴¹I receive not honour from men.

⁴²But I know you, that ye have not the love of God in you.

⁴³I am come in my Father's name, and ye receive me not: if another shall come in his own name, him ye will receive.

⁴⁴How can ye believe, which receive honour one of another, and seek not the honour that *cometh* from God only?

⁴⁵Do not think that I will accuse you to the Father: there is *one* that accuseth you, *even* Moses, in whom ye trust.

⁴⁶For had ye believed Moses, ye would have believed me: for he wrote of me.

Chapter five: Happiness is Undying

people in this way, as the very proof of the existence of your own inner aware-joy. Yet still many of you doubt.

41. "Many people still do not recognize the presence of their own inner happiness, which is their ordinary awareness, and thus they do not recognize or honor me.

42. "Still, even if you doubt it, your inner joy, this inner love, is in fact in you. It is you. I know this absolutely.

43. "I point to the joy in you and many of you resist looking, resist the notion itself. But when someone points to joy and happiness in the outer world, in some outer form or relationship or acquisition, this seems more believable. The outer forms are more acceptable to more people.

44. "Most people in the world are running after the outer happiness, the outer forms and relationships and acquisitions which they assume will make them happy. But the happiness they seek outwardly is already within them. Most people are simply ignoring that peace, that love, that joy that is already present at their core.

45. "Now don't be mistaken: I am not unhappy with you. It is impossible for me to be unhappy. Happiness is my nature, just as it is your nature. I am here simply pointing out the way things are for many people. I have great compassion for those suffering from misunderstandings of the nature and location of happiness. The scriptures of all cultures have all been pointing you to the same truths, the same happiness to which I am also now pointing.

46. "If you had studied the scriptures, followed their promptings, you would recognize that what I am now showing you is in fact true. What I am showing you here in my own flesh can be found in all the scriptures. What you see in me is what all the scriptures have affirmed to be the true nature of every human being.

⁴⁷But if ye believe not his writings, how shall ye believe my words?

Chapter 6

¹After these things Jesus went over the sea of Galilee, which is *the sea* of Tiberias.

²And a great multitude followed him, because they saw his miracles which he did on them that were diseased. ⁶And this he said to prove him: for he himself knew what he would do.

³And Jesus went up into a mountain, and there he sat with his disciples.

⁴And the passover, a feast of the Jews, was nigh.

⁵When Jesus then lifted up *his* eyes, and saw a great company come unto him, he saith unto Philip, Whence shall we buy bread, that these may eat?

47. "If you don't believe the scriptures, you probably won't believe me. But just look, and see for yourself if what is in you is what I say is there."

Chapter 6

1. After Jesus had shared all these insights and teachings with the people, he once again left with his friends and went into the neighboring countryside. They traveled a fairly good distance from where he had been teaching.

2. Nevertheless, a large group of people followed him because his teaching, and his very presence generated a powerful healing effect on those who heard. People were discovering they had been healed of all kinds of troubles.

3. Wanting the people to realize that it was their own inner connection with joy, with spirit or love that was healing them and not him personally, Jesus continued moving and went up into the mountains accompanied by a few close friends.

4. It happened to be another day of celebration and remembrance for the people of that tribe.

5. The people, of course, continued to follow Jesus because of the amazing things that were happening around him. Jesus looked at the large crowd of people who were there with him and his friends there in the wilderness on the mountain. He smiled, and asked Phillip, one of his close

⁶And this he said to prove him: for he himself knew what he would do.

⁷Philip answered him, Two hundred pennyworth of bread is not sufficient for them, that every one of them may take a little.

⁸One of his disciples, Andrew, Simon Peter's brother, saith unto him,

⁹There is a lad here, which hath five barley loaves, and two small fishes: but what are they among so many?

¹⁰And Jesus said, Make the men sit down. Now there was much grass in the place. So the men sat down, in number about five thousand.

¹¹And Jesus took the loaves; and when he had given thanks, he distributed to the disciples, and the disciples to them that were set down; and likewise of the fishes as much as they would.

friends, "How do you suppose we're going to feed all these folks? Is there a market close by?"

6. Jesus knew, of course, that there weren't any markets nearby. He also knew what was about to happen.

7. Phillip started to worry. "Even if there were markets nearby," Phillip said, "which there aren't, but even if there were, do you know how much it would cost to feed all these people?"

8. Andrew, Simon Peter's brother, another of Jesus' close friends, chimed in.

9. "A young boy here brought a few loaves of bread and a few fish. That seems to be the only food available. Actually, to be exact, he brought five loaves of bread and two fish. And they're very small fish, sad to say. But obviously, we have a huge crowd here. I can't see what good this boy's little bit of food will do us."

10. Jesus wasn't worried. "Have the people sit down," he said. They had all gathered in a large grassy meadow there on the mountain. The crowd had grown to about five thousand people.

11. Jesus took the bread that the young boy had brought and for a few moments held it, and was happy with it. He was completely at peace with it, knowing it, too, to be happiness itself. And he gave the bread to his friends and told them to pass it out to the people there in the meadow.

[12] When they were filled, he said unto his disciples, Gather up the fragments that remain, that nothing be lost.

[13] Therefore they gathered *them* together, and filled twelve baskets with the fragments of the five barley loaves, which remained over and above unto them that had eaten.

[14] Then those men, when they had seen the miracle that Jesus did, said, This is of a truth that prophet that should come into the world.

[15] When Jesus therefore perceived that they would come and take him by force, to make him a king, he departed again into a mountain himself alone.

And then Jesus did the same thing with the two small fish, being glad, happy with this little food. He was not worried. And then he gave the fish to his friends to also distribute among the people.

12. Curiously, the people ate and ate. And after they had eaten Jesus asked his friends to collect what was left over. "Don't want to waste anything," he said, smiling.

13. And when his friends started collecting what the people had not eaten, they were amazed, because what had started out as a few fish and five loaves of bread had somehow, after everybody had eaten, turned into twelve baskets of left-overs!

14. His friends then, once again, looked at Jesus with new eyes. They realized that the happiness that was working through this man, the happiness with which this man was completely identified, apparently had no limitations, no end to its wondrous unfolding.

15. Jesus realized what his own friends and the people on the mountain were thinking—that the happiness working here in him was something special and unique. Jesus realized that rather than honoring the happiness that was working in him, and working in everybody, they wanted to put him, as a person, on a pedestal. Jesus saw that they wanted to make him their boss, their leader, their savior. That they would insist on it. So he told them to stay put while he quietly slipped away, and walked by himself up higher on the mountain.

¹⁶And when even was *now* come, his disciples went down unto the sea,

¹⁷And entered into a ship, and went over the sea toward Capernaum. And it was now dark, and Jesus was not come to them.

¹⁸And the sea arose by reason of a great wind that blew.

¹⁹So when they had rowed about five and twenty or thirty furlongs, they see Jesus walking on the sea, and drawing nigh unto the ship: and they were afraid.

²⁰But he saith unto them, It is I; be not afraid.

²¹Then they willingly received him into the ship: and immediately the ship was at the land whither they went.

²²The day following, when the people which stood on the other side of the sea saw that there was none other boat there, save that one whereinto his disciples were entered, and that Jesus went not with his disciples into the boat, but *that* his disciples were gone away alone;

16. That evening his friends, assuming Jesus wanted to still be alone, went back down the mountain to the seashore.

17. It grew later and later, and the sun went down and still Jesus had not come down from the mountain. His friends had to attend to some business in a village further up the coast, so they chartered a boat to take them. They set out on their journey, without seeing hide nor hair of Jesus.

18. As they were sailing, a huge storm suddenly came up, accompanied by very high winds. This was unexpected.

19. When they were three or four miles out to sea, and the storm was raging, they saw someone walking across the water toward their boat. The figure kept walking their way. This spooked them, of course, and made them very afraid.

20. "Hey friends, it's me," Jesus finally said. "No need to be afraid."

21. They quickly helped him on board, and, curiously, once he was on board, they discovered that they were suddenly at the dock by the village where they were wanting to go.

22. The next day the people of the village saw that only one new boat had come ashore that night—the one in which Jesus' friends had set out. But the people back at the village they had just left knew that Jesus had not gone on the boat with his friends.

²³(Howbeit there came other boats from Tiberias nigh unto the place where they did eat bread, after that the Lord had given thanks:)

²⁴When the people therefore saw that Jesus was not there, neither his disciples, they also took shipping, and came to Capernaum, seeking for Jesus.

²⁵And when they had found him on the other side of the sea, they said unto him, Rabbi, when camest thou hither?

²⁶Jesus answered them and said, Verily, verily, I say unto you, Ye seek me, not because ye saw the miracles, but because ye did eat of the loaves, and were filled.

²⁷Labour not for the meat which perisheth, but for that meat which endureth unto everlasting life, which the Son of man shall give unto you: for him hath God the Father sealed.

Chapter Six: We Are Always Nourished by Joy

²³· In the village by the mountain where the day before Jesus had talked and given all the people bread and fishes, another group of people from up country had arrived. They had heard about all the miracles that were happening around Jesus.

²⁴· But since neither Jesus nor his friends were there, most of them chartered boats and sailed across the sea to follow Jesus and his friends in the new village.

²⁵· When the people finally found them, they asked Jesus, "Sir, friend, teacher, tell us, how in the world did you get here?"

²⁶· Jesus, seeing all the people from the day before, didn't answer the question. "You didn't come to find me because you understood about the happiness that I teach, that I am —the happiness that has no limitations of time and space, and that reveals that you are inherently whole, full and complete right where you are. You came to find me simply because you're hoping for more miracles, or more of the bread and fishes that you were given yesterday.

²⁷· "I'll tell you again. You already have nourishment within, close at hand, that you don't need to search for. Your inner food is always fresh, never spoils or rots or molds. Your inner nourishment is the joy within, the love, the light within you. You don't need to look outward for your sustenance. The awareness within is life itself, nourishment itself. I'm happy to demonstrate it for you, in my own life, but you, too, can find it and demonstrate it in

[28] Then said they unto him, What shall we do, that we might work the works of God?

[29] Jesus answered and said unto them, This is the work of God, that ye believe on him whom he hath sent.

[30] They said therefore unto him, What sign shewest thou then, that we may see, and believe thee? what dost thou work?

[31] Our fathers did eat manna in the desert; as it is written, He gave them bread from heaven to eat.

[32] Then Jesus said unto them, Verily, verily, I say unto you, Moses gave you not that bread from heaven; but my Father giveth you the true bread from heaven.

your own lives, because this inner light, this aware happiness, is what life gives and guarantees to each of us."

28. So the people asked him what they could do to have the miracles of happiness appear in their own lives.

29. "Listen to the happiness there inside you," Jesus said. "The happiness, the joy, the love there inside you will lead you, teach you, fulfill you more than anything you will ever find on the outside."

30. Jesus, of course, was on the outside of them and they still had their attention stuck on him as an outside person rather than the teaching he had come to share. "How do we know what you say is true?" they asked him. "What signs can you give us to show that what you are saying is really the way things are?

31. "Our scriptures are full of miracles, like bread appearing from heaven, to prove the truth of their teachings. So what will you do?" Apparently they had already forgotten or had just not put into context the bread that had appeared and fed them when they were on the side of the mountain.

32. Jesus said, "The true bread doesn't come from the scriptures. The scriptures only point you to the bread. The true nourishment comes from within, and is only confirmed outwardly by what you find in the scriptures.

[33] For the bread of God is he which cometh down from heaven, and giveth life unto the world.

[34] Then said they unto him, Lord, evermore give us this bread.

[35] And Jesus said unto them, I am the bread of life: he that cometh to me shall never hunger; and he that believeth on me shall never thirst.

[36] But I said unto you, That ye also have seen me, and believe not.

[37] All that the Father giveth me shall come to me; and him that cometh to me I will in no wise cast out.

33. "What the scriptures point to is already inside of you. This love, this joy, this awareness that is already there inside you is the bread that truly feeds and nourishes your life. In fact, your joy is the bread of life. Joy is life itself."

34. The people then said, please, friend, give us some of this bread.

35. Jesus let out a deep breath, and patiently explained it to them again. "Your awareness is your bread. I have demonstrated to you that it is possible for a person to release all false identities, all the accumulated, limited, time locked identities and live simply as happiness itself. You can see the happiness in me. You can see the results of living this happiness in this way. When you have dropped all the false identities, you rediscover the identity that never goes hungry and never gets thirsty.

36. "I have shown you how this inner happiness works. I have explained the inner joy to you and demonstrated it for you. But still, many of you continue to look outward rather than inward for your fullness, your completeness.

37. "The happiness that I have demonstrated for you is the same happiness already inside you. What I have shown you—the results of living in this way—is your own birthright. Anybody that turns to their own awareness, to inner happiness, to love, will surely find it there, and discover again the infinite, eternal nature of life.

³⁸For I came down from heaven, not to do mine own will, but the will of him that sent me.

³⁹And this is the Father's will which hath sent me, that of all which he hath given me I should lose nothing, but should raise it up again at the last day.

⁴⁰And this is the will of him that sent me, that every one which seeth the Son, and believeth on him, may have everlasting life: and I will raise him up at the last day.

⁴¹The Jews then murmured at him, because he said, I am the bread which came down from heaven.

38. "I am in no way different than any of you, except that I have allowed the inner awareness to be my very life. I allow awareness to think for me, speak for me, move me, breathe me, live me. It's the most natural way of living.

39. "Living as happiness, as awareness, I discovered, as you will discover, that everything was available to me, when I need it. The past and the future are available to me. All things rise and fall away but I, as awareness, am always right here, right now, full and complete and lacking absolutely nothing. I am awareness itself, happiness itself, love itself. Everything rises and falls in me, in this awareness, and yet this awareness never fades. I never lack a single thing.

40. "This will be your experience too, when you recognize that your very own awareness is the happiness I've been talking about. Not the things that rise up and fall away in awareness but the awareness itself is your joy. It's that which has been in you, and is you, and never goes away, even when the body is no more. As you outgrow your identification with the body, and no longer identify with the things and relationships and energies that rise and fall in awareness, and instead recognize your true identity as awareness itself, which in itself is love, is happiness, you'll discover yourself back home, at one with your simple, pure, never born, and never dying presence."

41. The elders of his tribe who were present felt threatened and offended with Jesus' radical teaching. Jesus claimed to be identified with happiness itself, love itself, and told

⁴²And they said, Is not this Jesus, the son of Joseph, whose father and mother we know? how is it then that he saith, I came down from heaven

⁴³Jesus therefore answered and said unto them, Murmur not among yourselves.

⁴⁴No man can come to me, except the Father which hath sent me draw him: and I will raise him up at the last day.

⁴⁵It is written in the prophets, And they shall be all taught of God. Every man therefore that hath heard, and hath learned of the Father, cometh unto me.

others they were at root already in the same condition. The elders held to the belief that there were traditions that needed to be followed, penances that needed to be paid, efforts needing to be made before one was complete, whole, loving.

42. So the elders spoke to the people there, and said, "Now don't get too carried away here. This fellow is not necessarily who he says he is. We actually know his parents, we know his upbringing. He is in fact just a regular Joe from the neighborhood. Nothing special. Nothing extraordinary. But here he is telling us he's happiness itself. Love itself. How could that happen, to just a regular Joe from the neighborhood?"

43. Jesus smiled, shook his head. "Please, there's no need to argue or be upset with each other because of me," he said.

44. "Just listen to your own hearts, listen to whether the happiness inside you resonates with what I'm saying. If your own awareness feels uplifted by these words, then you know what I am pointing to is real. It's that awareness that will be with you even after you drop the body. So stick with it. It's what's real.

45. "Your true teacher, your first guide is your own inner joy. All the scriptures point to this. When you are listening to your own heart, you are hearing what I'm saying. We are on the same path. We are traveling together.

⁴⁶Not that any man hath seen the Father, save he which is of God, he hath seen the Father.

⁴⁷Verily, verily, I say unto you, He that believeth on me hath everlasting life.

⁴⁸I am that bread of life.

⁴⁹Your fathers did eat manna in the wilderness, and are dead.

⁵⁰This is the bread which cometh down from heaven, that a man may eat thereof, and not die.

⁵¹I am the living bread which came down from heaven: if any man eat of this bread, he shall live for ever: and the bread that I will give is my flesh, which I will give for the life of the world.

Chapter Six: We Are Always Nourished by Joy

⁴⁶· "When you feel the love inside you, feel the joy, which is your basic awareness, you are feeling the life that is never born and never dies. That joy inside you is the same joy that is the origin and design of the universe, and yet is not affected by the coming and going of the universe.

⁴⁷· "So when you see through and let go of all your other identities and rest in your first identity, which is that love, that awareness, that joy, then you, too, are no longer affected by the coming and going of life's forms. Instead, you are always simply present with life itself, as life itself.

⁴⁸· "I know this because I have experienced it myself. I am experiencing it right now. I always experience it. I've discovered that I am happiness itself, just as you are happiness itself. I live my life this way. You can too.

⁴⁹· "For the most part, our parents and grandparents did not teach us this truth about the inner light, primarily because they themselves were not clear about it. And so their happiness comes and goes. Their joy is for the most part determined by outer circumstances.

⁵⁰· "What I am pointing towards is the happiness that is always present and available no matter the circumstances. It is a joy that is with you, that sustains and nourishes you, even when the physical body has dropped away.

⁵¹· "I am here with you as the living proof of that joy. Simply listening to my testimony is itself a part of the process of discovering the joy within you. As more and

[52] The Jews therefore strove among themselves, saying, How can this man give us *his* flesh to eat?

[53] Then Jesus said unto them, Verily, verily, I say unto you, Except ye eat the flesh of the Son of man, and drink his blood, ye have no life in you.

[54] Whoso eateth my flesh, and drinketh my blood, hath eternal life; and I will raise him up at the last day.

more of us recognize the life that is within us, the love, the joy that is in us, and live it here in our daily lives, then together we advance the cause of peace and harmony in the world. Our ordinary lives shine out as testimony to others, giving evidence of that presence that never dies. Abiding in that joy, as that joy, is the greatest service we can perform here on earth. The joy that flows through us, out of us, nourishes the world."

52. Hearing his words, the elders of the tribe once again mumbled amongst themselves. How are we supposed to nourish the world, they asked, just by being ourselves? Surely it can't be as simple as this.

53. Jesus replied, "If you aren't deeply aware of your own inner joy, if you don't make it your daily, even hourly focus of attention, constantly imbibing in it and spontaneously releasing it, you lose your sense of connection with life itself. Nothing feeds you or sustains you like awareness itself, which is even now radiating in and around you as the essence of your being.

54. "When you have seen through and let go of all your accumulated outer identities and are clear about your first, most natural and original identity—which is awareness itself—you are no longer frightened of death, and thus no longer frightened at all. And then you can be of true service in the world. When you have come home to your joy you have come home to the life which is both unborn and undying, yet supremely ordinary, loving and kind.

⁵⁵For my flesh is meat indeed, and my blood is drink indeed.

⁵⁶He that eateth my flesh, and drinketh my blood, dwelleth in me, and I in him.

⁵⁷As the living Father hath sent me, and I live by the Father: so he that eateth me, even he shall live by me.

⁵⁸This is that bread which came down from heaven: not as your fathers did eat manna, and are dead: he that eateth of this bread shall live for ever.

Chapter Six: We Are Always Nourished by Joy

55. "The inner happiness that you are attracts everything you need in the outer world. That is why I say your happiness is your meat and your drink.

56. "Our awareness— this inner light, happiness that we all share—is our common ground. As you get deeper into this you will discover that there is only one awareness, of which we are all expressions. When we rest in our own awareness we recognize ourselves in every other living form, and we discover every living form within us. We discover that the universe is one living body, and that our awareness reveals our place in it.

57. "What I am sharing here with you is what happiness has shown to me. Happiness guides me, animates me, is my very breath and heartbeat. The words I speak are brought out of me by the happiness that is within you. We are one process, one unfolding artistry. Your happiness needs me to be reminding you of this, and my happiness needs you to be hearing this. It is the same happiness, unfolding itself in ever-more beautiful ways.

58. "Although this teaching about our inner happiness is very simple and straightforward and easy to understand, it is not, generally, the teaching that was handed down to us by our fathers and grandfathers and the long traditions of human effort and struggle. That old tradition says we must find more life in something, or someone, or some belief system outside of what is already naturally inside of us. Such teachings have often led to a constant state of low level unhappiness and outer lives often filled with tragedy

⁵⁹These things said he in the synagogue, as he taught in Capernaum.

⁶⁰Many therefore of his disciples, when they had heard *this*, said, This is an hard saying; who can hear it?

⁶¹When Jesus knew in himself that his disciples murmured at it, he said unto them, Doth this offend you?

⁶²*What* and if ye shall see the Son of man ascend up where he was before?

⁶³It is the spirit that quickeneth; the flesh profiteth nothing: the words that I speak unto you, *they* are spirit, and *they* are life.

and personal loss and chaos. Only when we have consciously reconnected with our inner happiness do we go beyond the limitations of our cultural strife and struggle. In joy, we discover our lives unfolding peaceably, gracefully, effortlessly, and our simple presence becomes a quiet blessing to everybody we encounter."

59. Jesus taught these things in the main meeting hall of the district.

60. His friends that were with him were a bit worried about such teachings, since they were so different from what anybody else had taught here in this meeting hall. His friends were worried that the local people would not be ready for such a direct and personal teaching of universal happiness.

61. Jesus could easily read his friends' hearts and minds. "Are you worried and offended by what I am teaching here?" he asked.

62. "Do you want me to leave, or maybe just disappear here in front of your eyes? My own happiness is not in need of these demonstrations, these teachings.

63. "Happiness is the essence of life. All these polite traditions and customs and political and religious practices are useless if they don't support and affirm our happiness. Your very bodies are designed for happiness, by happiness. But happiness doesn't come from the outside, by stimulating your senses. It comes from the inside. My

⁶⁴But there are some of you that believe not. For Jesus knew from the beginning who they were that believed not, and who should betray him.

⁶⁵And he said, Therefore said I unto you, that no man can come unto me, except it were given unto him of my Father.

⁶⁶From that *time* many of his disciples went back, and walked no more with him.

⁶⁷Then said Jesus unto the twelve, Will ye also go away?

⁶⁸Then Simon Peter answered him, Lord, to whom shall we go? thou hast the words of eternal life.

teaching and demonstration are given only to awaken and refresh that happiness that is already inside you.

64. "Most of you recognize what I am saying and are grateful for these reminders. Some of you, though, are offended by what I teach, and take me to be a heretic." Because of his attunement with timeless joy, Jesus could plainly see what was ahead, and who around him would play which part. But Jesus was not afraid of his destiny, or of the people who would play their parts in it.

65. Jesus said, "Those of you who recognize the truth of this happiness I'm pointing to are able to recognize it because it is the same happiness alive in you. It is your own happiness that resonates with the words I speak. Those of you who consider me a heretic, I would ask you to consider whether you might be denying your own inner reality, and mistaking the surface of life for its depths."

66. A number of people there, who had been attracted to him because of the bread and fishes he had given out on the mountain, now decided to leave. They felt offended by his teaching, so a fairly large group of them went away.

67. Jesus looked at those close friends still around him and asked, "How about you? Are you also ready to leave?"

68. Then one of his best friends, Simon Peter, said, "Where on earth could we go where we could find as much life and joy and peace as we find right here, with you? You have showed us the essence of being, which never dies.

⁶⁹And we believe and are sure that thou art that Christ, the Son of the living God.

⁷⁰Jesus answered them, Have not I chosen you twelve, and one of you is a devil?

⁷¹He spake of Judas Iscariot *the son* of Simon: for he it was that should betray him, being one of the twelve.

Chapter 7

¹After these things Jesus walked in Galilee: for he would not walk in Jewry, because the Jews sought to kill him.

⁶⁹. "We can say without doubt that your teaching about joy is true because we have experienced it, experienced you, and we will never again be the same. You have shown us that awareness does not come and go with the outer circumstances, but is with us always."

⁷⁰· Jesus smiled. "Yes, thank you Peter. You are my true friends. You do see what I am pointing to. You do experience the reality of your own awareness, or happiness. At least most of you do. And I'm grateful for that. Just so you know, however, I see that that one of you is still deeply convinced that happiness will only come someday in the future from the outside. One of you is staying here with me under false pretenses."

⁷¹· He was of course, talking about poor Judas Iscariot, who was destined to play his own lonely role in mankind's unfolding story. Judas would try to betray happiness itself.

Chapter 7

¹. Jesus knew that people's reactions to the things he was saying were growing extreme. For some, his teachings were life changing. For others, they were life threatening because they challenged their very identities. In fact, some people's reactions were so extreme that they were ready to have him killed. For the most part, Jesus in his travels intentionally stayed away from the areas where the people had such an adverse response.

²Now the Jews' feast of tabernacles was at hand.

³His brethren therefore said unto him, Depart hence, and go into Judaea, that thy disciples also may see the works that thou doest.

⁴For *there is* no man *that* doeth any thing in secret, and he himself seeketh to be known openly. If thou do these things, shew thyself to the world.

⁵For neither did his brethren believe in him.

⁶Then Jesus said unto them, My time is not yet come: but your time is alway ready.

⁷The world cannot hate you; but me it hateth, because I testify of it, that the works thereof are evil.

2. Nevertheless, there was another traditional yearly celebration coming up where all the people of his tribe were expected to gather.

3. His friends encouraged him to continue his public speaking and demonstrations of happiness. "You should go to the celebration," his friends said. "Nobody has ever shown the effects of happiness, of love, the way you do. People there will be grateful for all the healing that takes place wherever you go.

4. "You should go there and show people what you can do. If you're like us, you want everybody to know what great things you can do. Nobody wants to be ignored. Since all these amazing things happen around you, surely you want others to see you can do these wonderful things."

5. Sadly, his friends were encouraging him this way because secretly they just needed more outer proofs of his happiness teaching.

6. "I don't feel the need to demonstrate anything," Jesus said. "These things happen in their own time. Any of you could as easily demonstrate the truth of this teaching right now, right here. Just practice love right where you are.

7. "Others won't resent you and hold your practice against you as they often do towards me. My teaching and demonstration of happiness reveals to them their own unhappiness. They hold to their unhappiness and even magnify it to argue against me.

⁸Go ye up unto this feast: I go not up yet unto this feast; for my time is not yet full come.

⁹When he had said these words unto them, he abode *still* in Galilee.

¹⁰But when his brethren were gone up, then went he also up unto the feast, not openly, but as it were in secret.

¹¹Then the Jews sought him at the feast, and said, Where is he?

¹²And there was much murmuring among the people concerning him: for some said, He is a good man: others said, Nay; but he deceiveth the people.

¹³Howbeit no man spake openly of him for fear of the Jews.

¹⁴Now about the midst of the feast Jesus went up into the temple, and taught.

Chapter Seven: Practice Love Right Where You Are

8. "So you people go on up to the celebration. I myself am going to hold back, stay away. It's just not time yet for me to continue demonstrating this teaching so publicly."

9. When Jesus said these things to his friends they were all still hanging out by the seashore.

10. So his friends left to go on to the celebration, and then Jesus, by himself, quietly followed. He was willing to go to the celebration, but he wanted to be fairly anonymous.

11. At the celebration a lot of the people asked Jesus' friends about him. Where is he, they asked.

12. Some of the people wanted to know where he was because they had been so impressed, and moved and uplifted by his teachings. Others wanted to know where he was because they were the ones who wanted to do him harm, because they thought he was threatening their traditions and leading people astray.

13. At this point, Jesus' friends were not standing up and openly supporting or defending him. They were all still afraid of those in the tribe who were ready to hurt him. His friends worried that they themselves would be in danger if they spoke up in his defense.

14. Having slipped in unnoticed, Jesus found himself again in the middle of the crowd and happily, spontaneously sharing what he knew, what he was with those around

¹⁵And the Jews marvelled, saying, How knoweth this man letters, having never learned?

¹⁶Jesus answered them, and said, My doctrine is not mine, but his that sent me.

¹⁷If any man will do his will, he shall know of the doctrine, whether it be of God, or *whether* I speak of myself.

¹⁸He that speaketh of himself seeketh his own glory: but he that seeketh his glory that sent him, the same is true, and no unrighteousness is in him.

him. And again, more and more people began to gather to listen.

15. And the elders of the tribe were once again amazed. "How can this guy talk this way," they asked, "about these things that are really none of his business? They are things only we have been ordained to talk about. He hasn't gone through our training, or been on the leadership track."

16. Jesus smiled and said, "It's not my personal teaching that I'm offering or personal energy that I'm sharing. It's the teaching and energy of awareness itself, of joy, of love. I have no choice. It's who I am. It's what naturally flows through me.

17. "In fact, however, I'm no different than any of you. Look within and feel the joy, the love, the awareness that is always there behind all the mind stuff that generally fogs up your true nature. Just look behind the mind stuff. You will know for yourselves that what I say is true.

18. "If I was just blowing my own horn and hoping to be somebody special, that would be one thing. You would have a case against me. Yet I'm not here blowing my own horn. Rather I'm just pointing to the wonder, the power, the magnificence that is in each of us. When we blow our own horns we are shallow and silly and without substance. When we express the single life, the single joy that we all share, we are being of service to the world.

[19] Did not Moses give you the law, and *yet* none of you keepeth the law? Why go ye about to kill me?

[20] The people answered and said, Thou hast a devil: who goeth about to kill thee?

[21] Jesus answered and said unto them, I have done one work, and ye all marvel.

[22] Moses therefore gave unto you circumcision; (not because it is of Moses, but of the fathers;) and ye on the sabbath day circumcise a man.

[23] If a man on the sabbath day receive circumcision, that the law of Moses should not be broken; are ye angry at me, because I have made a man every whit whole on the sabbath day?

[24] Judge not according to the appearance, but judge righteous judgment.

Chapter Seven: Practice Love Right Where You Are   101

19. "All of our traditions, and scriptures are pointing to the exact thing I'm talking about. Undying joy, love, awareness is within each of us. So why are some of you so upset with me, even wanting to kill me?"

20. His words surprised some of the people. "What do you mean? Who wants to kill you? Nobody wants to kill you. You're just being paranoid."

21. Jesus didn't argue. He just shook his head. "You are all amazed that the happiness that moves through me has expressed itself in a few healings and feedings. And specifically the healing of that fellow that occurred on what our tradition calls a holy day.

22. "Look at all the crazy things that we do in the meeting house on holy days, including ancient songs and personal rituals and communal chanting. These are just a few of the things our traditions lead us to do that are intended to cleanse and purify and uplift us in some way or another.

23. "If all these things are okay to do on the holy day, why would anybody be angry with me if on that same day I had a hand in helping some poor fellow to shake off years of infirmity and in one beautiful moment finally stand up and walk?

24. "Don't just look at the surface of things, whether somebody is performing all the rituals and saying all the right words and conforming to the way tradition would instruct us to do. Look underneath the forms to the

²⁵Then said some of them of Jerusalem, Is not this he, whom they seek to kill?

²⁶But, lo, he speaketh boldly, and they say nothing unto him. Do the rulers know indeed that this is the very Christ?

²⁷Howbeit we know this man whence he is: but when Christ cometh, no man knoweth whence he is.

²⁸Then cried Jesus in the temple as he taught, saying, Ye both know me, and ye know whence I am: and I am not come of myself, but he that sent me is true, whom ye know not.

²⁹But I know him: for I am from him, and he hath sent me.

³⁰Then they sought to take him: but no man laid hands on him, because his hour was not yet come.

²⁷Howbeit we know this man whence he is: but when Christ cometh, no man knoweth whence he is.

²⁸Then cried Jesus in the temple as he taught, saying, Ye both know me, and ye know whence I am: and I am not come of myself, but he that sent me is true, whom ye know not.

²⁹But I know him: for I am from him, and he hath sent me.

awareness that is there, the joy, the love. If that's there, that's what counts."

25. His words struck home, and because of his words the people again recognized him. "This is the fellow that they want to do away with," they said.

26. "But here he is, speaking openly and freely and without fear. This guy really is happiness itself, total happiness. Why don't the elders of our tribe recognize this?

27. "It seems we ourselves can recognize him as a man, and know his background and recognize the value of his teachings. But we are not yet able to demonstrate true happiness outside of this man's personal presence."

28. By this time they had all moved to the main meeting hall again. "You're exactly right," he said. "You know me as another human being, just like everybody else. What I am teaching, though, and what I am demonstrating does not come from just one more limited human being. The happiness that I teach and express is not limited. It is the very essence of all of life. This happiness, that is more than human opinion or sense stimulation, is something you have not yet understood and thus have not yet embodied in your daily lives.

29. "Nevertheless, I can confirm for you directly, that I myself have and do constantly experience this joyful essence of life, and fully embody it."

³⁰Then they sought to take him: but no man laid hands on him, because his hour was not yet come.

³¹And many of the people believed on him, and said, When Christ cometh, will he do more miracles than these which this *man* hath done?

³²The Pharisees heard that the people murmured such things concerning him; and the Pharisees and the chief priests sent officers to take him.

³³Then said Jesus unto them, Yet a little while am I with you, and *then* I go unto him that sent me.

³⁴Ye shall seek me, and shall not find *me*: and where I am, *thither* ye cannot come.

30. Jesus' bold words angered even more of the elders of the tribe, who assumed that teaching about the eternal essence of life, and claiming it as one's own, was not Jesus' prerogative. And Jesus' understanding of this essence was not the same as their own. Thus, they were even more eager to grab him and shut him up. But nobody touched him. Happiness itself had its own story to tell, and according to happiness itself, this was not the time for Jesus to be taken away.

31. Many of the people there in the meeting hall were convinced of the truth of Jesus' words. "What more proof do we need, or what greater things should we expect, than the healing and harmonizing miracles that we have already witnessed in this man's presence?"

32. Again the elders of the tribe heard the people talking in this way, praising and believing the words and works of Jesus. The elders decided enough was enough and they sent some security men to take Jesus away.

33. Jesus said to the security men, "I am here demonstrating for you the nature of unlimited happiness. Seasons change. Happiness itself will take this body away before long.

34. "At that point you will want to come find me for a different reason, to fulfill your own joy. Looking outward, though, you won't be able to find me. Looking outward, you won't be able to come to where I am."

[35] Then said the Jews among themselves, Whither will he go, that we shall not find him? will he go unto the dispersed among the Gentiles, and teach the Gentiles?

[36] What *manner of* saying is this that he said, Ye shall seek me, and shall not find *me*: and where I am, *thither* ye cannot come?

[37] In the last day, that great *day* of the feast, Jesus stood and cried, saying, If any man thirst, let him come unto me, and drink.

[38] He that believeth on me, as the scripture hath said, out of his belly shall flow rivers of living water.

[39] (But this spake he of the Spirit, which they that believe on him should receive: for the Holy Ghost was not yet *given*; because that Jesus was not yet glorified.)

35. The disbelievers of the tribe, those who still did not grasp what he was pointing to, asked, "Where could he possibly go that we can't find him? Is he saying that he is going to leave this area and go to other tribes, other nations, and teach there?

36. "And even if he did go to other areas and other tribes, why couldn't we go see him there? What did he mean when he said that we won't be able to go to where he is?"

37. As usual, the celebration continued for several days. On the last day, Jesus stood and again shared his simple message. "Turn to your inner awareness," he said, "to your inner love, to joy, for whatever outer need you have. Your solution is always waiting for you there inside you. I know, because I've learned that our inner awareness is the universal happiness. Our inner love is the universal love. There is no difference. I have learned to dwell in happiness itself, love itself. I encourage you to do the same.

38. "When you turn your attention to the love, joy, awareness that resides as your deepest self, you will discover all the riches of the world pouring forth and appearing in and around you. Turning within, you will discover, just as all the scriptures have promised, that living presence that never fades, never diminishes, is ever available and abundant and is more than sufficient to meet all of your outer needs."

39. Jesus' pointing to the powers of life and love and joy that are immediately available to every human being, without

⁴⁰Many of the people therefore, when they heard this saying, said, Of a truth this is the Prophet.

⁴¹Others said, This is the Christ. But some said, Shall Christ come out of Galilee?

⁴²Hath not the scripture said, That Christ cometh of the seed of David, and out of the town of Bethlehem, where David was?

⁴³So there was a division among the people because of him.

⁴⁴And some of them would have taken him; but no man laid hands on him.

an intermediary, was in direct contradiction to the rituals and superstitions of not only his time but of most of human history. He was pointing to a timeless truth that he himself would soon demonstrate in its fullness.

40. Many of the people who heard him speak this way resonated deeply with the light he was sharing. They recognized him as one who was expressing quite clearly, in new ways, for his time, the ancient truths contained in the scriptures.

41. Still other recognized him as pure joy, undiluted love, the essence of life showing itself in a human being. But others, of course, doubted. What Jesus was teaching and demonstrating seemed too good to be true. And besides, how could an untrained local boy know the scriptures so well and express their principles in this new way?

42. So some of the people started nit-picking about what the scriptures said and didn't say, and what their traditions demanded of them and predicted for the tribe.

43. So they were arguing amongst themselves, and tempers were heating up about the truth or falsity of Jesus' teachings.

44. Some of them became so angry with what Jesus had been saying that they were ready to grab him, take him away, although nobody did, not even the security people who had been sent.

⁴⁵Then came the officers to the chief priests and Pharisees; and they said unto them, Why have ye not brought him?

⁴⁶The officers answered, Never man spake like this man.

⁴⁷Then answered them the Pharisees, Are ye also deceived?

⁴⁸Have any of the rulers or of the Pharisees believed on him?

⁴⁹But this people who knoweth not the law are cursed.

⁵⁰Nicodemus saith unto them, (he that came to Jesus by night, being one of them,)

⁵¹Doth our law judge *any* man, before it hear him, and know what he doeth?

⁵²They answered and said unto him, Art thou also of Galilee? Search, and look: for out of Galilee ariseth no prophet.

45. These security people went back to the leaders of the tribe and the leaders asked, "Where is he? Why haven't you brought him in?"

46. The security people said, "We've never heard anybody talk so pure and simple and happy like this fellow does."

47. The elders of the tribe grumbled, and were irritated. "Have you all also been fooled by this man?" they asked.

48. "We people with authority—we chiefs and politicians and priests—don't believe him, so why should you?

49. "Only you people who aren't formally trained in the law, or in the scriptures or traditions are moved by this man's teachings and healings. He will lead these common people into trouble, just watch."

50. One of the security people they were saying this to was a fellow named Nicodemus. Nicodemus had been secretly going to hear Jesus whenever he could.

51. "Does our legal tradition allow us to find a man guilty before we even listen to his testimony or hear his side of the story? Can we find him guilty before we see him in action?"

52. The elders looked at Nicodemus and said, "So you're one of his group, right? You're also a local boy, telling us what is right and what's wrong in our traditions. If you knew anything you'd know that it's simply not possible

⁵³And every man went unto his own house.

Chapter 8

¹Jesus went unto the mount of Olives.

²And early in the morning he came again into the temple, and all the people came unto him; and he sat down, and taught them.

³And the scribes and Pharisees brought unto him a woman taken in adultery; and when they had set her in the midst,

⁴They say unto him, Master, this woman was taken in adultery, in the very act.

⁵Now Moses in the law commanded us, that such should be stoned: but what sayest thou?

⁶This they said, tempting him, that they might have to accuse him. But Jesus stooped down, and with *his* finger wrote on the ground, *as though he heard them not.*

for the locals to talk about these things with any kind of authority."

53. Nothing was resolved, so everybody just left things as they were and went back to their own homes.

Chapter 8

1. Jesus walked to a nearby mountain famous for its olive orchards. He went up the path away from the crowds.

2. He spent the day there, before coming back down that evening to the meeting hall. A large group of people gathered around him again, and he once again began to teach them.

3. Some of the elders still wanted to trap him into saying or doing something they could hold against him. They brought a woman to him who had been caught having intercourse with a man to whom she was not married.

4. "Okay, teacher man," they said to Jesus. "This woman was caught having sex with someone not her husband.

5. "Now as you know," they continued, "that's contrary to our culture and tradition and scripture. Our law says this a capital offense and would insist we put her to death."

6. Again, they were trying to trap him into saying something they could hold against him in a trial. Jesus looked at them, shook his head and then without saying

⁷So when they continued asking him, he lifted up himself, and said unto them, He that is without sin among you, let him first cast a stone at her.

⁸And again he stooped down, and wrote on the ground.

⁹And they which heard *it*, being convicted by *their own* conscience, went out one by one, beginning at the eldest, *even* unto the last: and Jesus was left alone, and the woman standing in the midst.

¹⁰When Jesus had lifted up himself, and saw none but the woman, he said unto her, Woman, where are those thine accusers? hath no man condemned thee?

anything simply knelt down and began making drawings in the dirt, as if he hadn't heard their questions.

7. But they continued pressing him on the issue, so he stood up and looked at each of them that were trying to trap him. "Is there anybody here who hasn't, at some point in your life, been unhappy, and then tried to find a little happiness in ways that may not have been acceptable to the wider community? If somebody here can say that they've never done this, that's who we will make both judge and executioner for this woman."

8. He looked around, and then again knelt and made drawings in the dirt.

9. And of course, there was nobody there who had not been unhappy at times, and at times had tried to remedy such unhappiness through un-thoughtful or inappropriate ways. Just the way Jesus said it made them see their own lives in new ways. So slowly most of those who had been hoping to trap him began to turn and leave, beginning with the leaders and the elders, and then their followers. As they left, Jesus kept writing in the dirt, and the woman stood there beside him.

10. When Jesus looked up and saw that most of those who had been trying to trap him had left, he stood. He smiled at the woman. "Friend," he said. "Can you see that we are all in this together? Can you see that at root we all share the same consciousness, the same awareness? No one is

[11] She said, No man, Lord. And Jesus said unto her, Neither do I condemn thee: go, and sin no more.

[12] Then spake Jesus again unto them, saying, I am the light of the world: he that followeth me shall not walk in darkness, but shall have the light of life.

[13] The Pharisees therefore said unto him, Thou bearest record of thyself; thy record is not true.

[14] Jesus answered and said unto them, Though I bear record of myself, *yet* my record is true: for I know whence I came, and whither I go; but ye cannot tell whence I come, and whither I go.

left outside this joy. Everyone is simply trying to get back to their own happiness."

11. "I can see that," the woman said. "When you asked if there was anybody who had not at one time been unhappy and had tried to foolishly remedy that unhappiness --- everybody understood what you meant." Jesus said, "Your happiness is always already here. Unhappiness always dissolves with this understanding. You can rest in your native happiness— in your natural awareness, your ordinary being--- and simply no longer identify with or give power to unhappiness."

12. Jesus spoke to the others there who had remained with him. "Happiness is the living light inside you," he said. "Stay with your happiness. It will light your path through the darkness. I know this because I myself have let go of all unhappiness and live as happiness itself. I'm here to show you that this can be done."

13. Some of the doubters questioned him on this. "You tell us that you are identified with happiness itself. But you appear to be just an ordinary man claiming something that seems impossible, incredible."

14. Jesus said, "I am not claiming anything. I'm just sharing with you what I know to be true. Happiness itself is my own nature, and it is yours too. Regardless of whether you believe me or not, happiness remains, in me and in you. I come from happiness and will return to happiness, just as you have come from happiness and will return to

[15]Ye judge after the flesh; I judge no man.

[16]And yet if I judge, my judgment is true: for I am not alone, but I and the Father that sent me.

[17]It is also written in your law, that the testimony of two men is true.

[18]I am one that bear witness of myself, and the Father that sent me beareth witness of me.

[19]Then said they unto him, Where is thy Father? Jesus answered, Ye neither know me, nor my Father: if ye had known me, ye should have known my Father also.

happiness. Your old habitual concepts and fearful feelings all rise up to obscure your direct observation of this.

15. "You judge these things with your old concepts and feelings, and thus limit yourself, and the people and circumstances around you. I stand in happiness itself and see happiness in its infinite variations.

16. "Everywhere I look, I see perfection. Awareness itself is perfect. It is the originator and sustainer of the universe. I rest in this awareness. I am this awareness. I'm here to show you this awareness. Awareness itself has sent me.

17. "Your own traditions support the principle that when two witnesses agree about the truth of some circumstance, then it can be accepted as probably true.

18. "Your awareness and my awareness and the universal awareness are the same awareness. If you can feel this, sense this interiorly, we have fulfilled the scripture, followed the law. Our happiness – this awareness right here, right now—is true. Awareness is the underlying reality of our lives."

19. Some of the doubters there said, "What happiness? Our reality doesn't contain much happiness. What are you talking about?" Jesus answered, "The happiness that I'm talking about, in me and in you, has always been there, is always there, yet nobody trusts it, nobody points it out. It's commonly overlooked because we are so busy looking for happiness in particular outer conditions and particular

[20] These words spake Jesus in the treasury, as he taught in the temple: and no man laid hands on him; for his hour was not yet come.

[21] Then said Jesus again unto them, I go my way, and ye shall seek me, and shall die in your sins: whither I go, ye cannot come.

[22] Then said the Jews, Will he kill himself? because he saith, Whither I go, ye cannot come.

people and particular things. Searching this way, you don't know your own happiness. You miss what is immediately available. You miss it in yourself, and thus you miss it in me, and everybody else."

20. Jesus was saying these things in the very middle of the meeting hall. This type of teaching, and his call to wake up had never occurred here before. Nobody tried to stop him, however, because there seemed to be an air of inevitability around him. He was doing what he needed to be doing for this time and place.

21. Jesus continued sharing his understanding. "Happiness moves on its own accord. Thus happiness moves me in harmony with perfect grace. When you try to find happiness on the outside, somewhere other than in your own inner being, that happiness will be fleeting. Even in me, where you have experienced happiness, if you come looking for me, looking for your happiness in me, you won't be able to find me. Unless you turn within and look for the joy that is there, you will be trapped by various forms of unhappiness time and again until the day you die. I've followed the inner prompting of joy. Until you do the same, you won't be able to follow me."

22. The elders were still stuck in their outer searches, clinging to their old world view. "What does he mean that we won't be able to find him, that we can't follow him where he goes? Is he saying he's going to kill himself or something?"

²³And he said unto them, Ye are from beneath; I am from above: ye are of this world; I am not of this world.

²⁴I said therefore unto you, that ye shall die in your sins: for if ye believe not that I am *he*, ye shall die in your sins.

²⁵Then said they unto him, Who art thou? And Jesus saith unto them, Even *the same* that I said unto you from the beginning.

²⁶I have many things to say and to judge of you: but he that sent me is true; and I speak to the world those things which I have heard of him.

²⁷They understood not that he spake to them of the Father.

²⁸Then said Jesus unto them, When ye have lifted up the Son of man, then shall ye know that I am *he*, and *that* I do nothing of myself; but as my Father hath taught me, I speak these things.

23. "Take your eyes off the forms off happiness and see the formless happiness," Jesus said. "You are still stuck in the appearance of things. Appearances come and go. Look behind the appearances.

24. "I cautioned that until you do this you will be stuck in unhappiness. I'm here teaching as clear and straight as I can. Take my prompting. Look behind the appearances. Find the joy, the beauty, the love that is behind the appearances, that is not affected by appearances. Otherwise, unhappiness will be your daily burden."

25. Then they asked him, again, how can you say these things? Who are you to be teaching this way? Jesus let out a deep breath. "I am happiness itself," he said. "Like I've been saying all along. I am that happiness that was here before the beginning of time. And so are you.

26. "It's easy for me to teach this way because it is happiness itself that is moving in me. The expressions of happiness are infinite, and yet happiness itself is singular. So the forms and manifestations of this teaching are ever-changing, yet the underlying love, the underlying joy never changes. It's that joy, that love that I share."

27. Still, most of the people there could not perceive that Jesus was talking to them about the very essence of all life.

28. He continued to bring their attention back to the basics of his teaching, again and again. "Honor the power and wisdom and grace of your own joy," he said, "Your inner

²⁹And he that sent me is with me: the Father hath not left me alone; for I do always those things that please him.

³⁰As he spake these words, many believed on him.

³¹Then said Jesus to those Jews which believed on him, If ye continue in my word, *then* are ye my disciples indeed;

³²And ye shall know the truth, and the truth shall make you free.

light, inner awareness , is the light of life. As you reconnect with that light, you connect with me, and what I am teaching here. There is only one light, one joy, and I am that light, that joy, just as you are that light, that joy. It is not me that is pointing this out. It is joy itself, awareness itself that speaks through me, for me. It is that awareness that animates us all.

[29.] "I am never without this awareness. Nor are you. It is what moves me, breathes me, sees through me, hears through me, just as it moves and breathes and sees and hears through you. Awareness is happy to do this, in all of us!"

[30.] Many people were starting to understand him now. It was not only the words he was speaking that helped them understand, but the love and joy and gentle confidence with which he spoke the words that helped them to directly feel what he was talking about.

[31.] Jesus recognized that the people were starting to understand. "This teaching, these words reveal how we are true friends to each other. As you practice this happiness you will discover that we are all in fact brothers and sisters in the same family.

[32.] "As you know and practice your happiness, you spontaneously grow increasingly free of all appearances of unhappiness, even the unhappiness of death itself."

³³They answered him, We be Abraham's seed, and were never in bondage to any man: how sayest thou, Ye shall be made free?

³⁴Jesus answered them, Verily, verily, I say unto you, Whosoever committeth sin is the servant of sin.

³⁵And the servant abideth not in the house for ever: *but* the Son abideth ever.

³⁶If the Son therefore shall make you free, ye shall be free indeed.

³⁷I know that ye are Abraham's seed; but ye seek to kill me, because my word hath no place in you.

33. Some of the people there argued with him. "But wait," they said, "most of our lives aren't so bad right now. Many of us inherited some nice properties or have accumulated property over the years, and most of us have fairly decent family lives, good diets, we're mostly healthy. So what do you mean we will grow increasingly free of unhappiness?"

34. Jesus replied, "I'm pointing to what you are holding in consciousness, in thought. If you continue to try to hold on to thoughts, either positive or negative, you will be caught by unhappiness, regardless of your outer circumstances. Most of us have not been taught to let go of our thoughts, so most people continually struggle with their thoughts, holding on or shoving them away. So they are caught by their thoughts and have become slaves to unhappiness, day after day, slaves to their thoughts..

35. "Fortunately, thoughts come and go, but awareness itself remains. As you allow your thoughts to come and go as they will, and simply rest in your awareness, your natural being, you experience your happiness, and draw closer to me, and this teaching I have come to share.

36. "It is this pre-thought awareness that is within you that sets you free of all unhappiness, first from the unhappiness of your own thoughts, and then from unhappiness in your outer circumstances.

37. "Those of you who continue to put your hope for happiness in following tradition and ritual and continually rearranging your inner and outer circumstances will resist

[38] I speak that which I have seen with my Father: and ye do that which ye have seen with your father.

[39] They answered and said unto him, Abraham is our father. Jesus saith unto them, If ye were Abraham's children, ye would do the works of Abraham.

[40] But now ye seek to kill me, a man that hath told you the truth, which I have heard of God: this did not Abraham.

[41] Ye do the deeds of your father. Then said they to him, We be not born of fornication; we have one Father, *even* God.

and deny this teaching, and even want me silenced permanently because of my challenge to your thinking, and your old ways of relating to your thoughts.

38. "Again, though, I tell you that it is happiness itself that is moving through me, speaking through me to you like this, even as you cling to your old unhappy ways of thinking and seeing."

39. The people responded by defending their ways. "This is the way we were taught," they said. "Our way of living, and striving after happiness, goes back for centuries." "Obviously, our old ways of thinking and living have lost something over the centuries," Jesus responded. "Otherwise, if those ways actually worked, you all would be experiencing much more happiness than you are experiencing today.

40. "But you're so unhappy with me, a man who simply points to the happiness that dwells within you, that many of you are ready to be my judge, jury and executioner. I am sharing the lessons of happiness that I have learned directly from happiness itself, not from tradition or ritual.

41. "But you cling to tradition and ritual, and tell me that this is not the way it should be done, not the way it should be taught." They continued to argue with him, telling him that they were in fact already practicing happiness through these old ways of thinking and acting, and these ways that have been handed down are more than sufficient.

⁴²Jesus said unto them, If God were your Father, ye would love me: for I proceeded forth and came from God; neither came I of myself, but he sent me.

⁴³Why do ye not understand my speech? *even* because ye cannot hear my word.

⁴⁴Ye are of *your* father the devil, and the lusts of your father ye will do. He was a murderer from the beginning, and abode not in the truth, because there is no truth in him. When he speaketh a lie, he speaketh of his own: for he is a liar, and the father of it.

42. Jesus sighed. "If you truly knew your own happiness, " he said, "if you were truly practicing happiness, living with it as a moment by moment experience, you would recognize me, and rejoice in this teaching. My happiness is your happiness. Your happiness is my happiness. It is one happiness. When I speak of happiness, I am not speaking just of my own. I am speaking of that happiness that is at the very root of all life.

43. "You continue to resist what I am pointing to here because you continue to have faith in some form of touchable happiness coming to you some day from outside, from some kind of outer relationship or circumstance or fortunate occurrence.

44. "Let me tell you straight out that such a faith in some future happiness—the faith in the future that you learned from tradition and ritual—is simply false. Such a faith inevitably perpetrates unhappiness, both in yourself and in others. Such a faith leads you to treating others as if they were trinkets or throw-away objects, and treating yourself the same, as if you had no worth. A faith in happiness arriving sometime in the future covers and smothers the happiness that is already present. Look at our communal history, which is the result of this faith. Can't you see the wars and sufferings, lies and deceits, unhappiness and pain that such a faith in the future has brought upon us? I'm telling you that your happiness is always and only right now. Clinging to your faith in some future happiness is clinging to a lie.

⁴⁵And because I tell *you* the truth, ye believe me not.

⁴⁶Which of you convinceth me of sin? And if I say the truth, why do ye not believe me?

⁴⁷He that is of God heareth God's words: ye therefore hear *them* not, because ye are not of God.

⁴⁸Then answered the Jews, and said unto him, Say we not well that thou art a Samaritan, and hast a devil?

⁴⁹Jesus answered, I have not a devil; but I honour my Father, and ye do dishonour me.

45. "And even now, when I tell you this, many of you still don't believe me. Many of you think that sometime in the future I will be proven wrong, and then your happiness— your future happiness— will deliver the final verdict against me.

46. "Can any of you point out any unhappiness arising here in me right now? If I am presenting happiness to you, why do you continue to resist it, deny it?"

47. Jesus smiled. "I know that many of you do in fact recognize this happiness, and experience your own uncaused joy when you are in my company. I have reminded you of something that has been there all along and with my words, you remember. Others of you continue to cover it over with your old habitual concepts and projections and prejudices. You cling to your thoughts and your unhappiness because this is what you have come to identify with."

48. This hit a sore spot for some of the people from the tribe. "We're doing just fine the way we are, thank you," they said. "You're the one that's unhappy. You've apparently identified yourself with some other tribe."

49. "No, I'm not unhappy," Jesus said. "And I've not identified with another tribe. You still don't see me clearly. I've rediscovered my first identity, my original identity, and that's with awareness itself. I observe that I am awareness itself, happiness itself.

⁵⁰And I seek not mine own glory: there is one that seeketh and judgeth.

⁵¹Verily, verily, I say unto you, If a man keep my saying, he shall never see death.

⁵²Then said the Jews unto him, Now we know that thou hast a devil. Abraham is dead, and the prophets; and thou sayest, If a man keep my saying, he shall never taste of death.

⁵³Art thou greater than our father Abraham, which is dead? and the prophets are dead: whom makest thou thyself?

⁵⁴Jesus answered, If I honour myself, my honour is nothing: it is my Father that honoureth me; of whom ye say, that he is your God:

⁵⁰. "This awareness, this happiness is not personal to me. It does not belong to me. It is the awareness, the happiness that pervades the entire universe, and keeps the harmony, the rhythms, the seen and unseen forces in balance.

⁵¹. "When you rest in this harmony, this awareness, this joy, forms rise and fall, even the forms of your own physical bodies, but you remain present, alive, undisturbed."

⁵². Some of the tribal leaders then said, "Now we know for sure you have gone off the deep end. Everybody we have ever known, including the first founders of our tribe, have all died, and gone away. Absolutely everybody, without exception. And here you come and tell us that if we follow your way of living that we won't go away, that we'll be here always.

⁵³. "Are you saying that your teaching, and this way of living, is better than anything that has ever come before? That you know the secret that nobody else has ever known? Who do you think you are?"

⁵⁴· Jesus shook his head. "Again, he said. "It's not me. It's happiness itself, peace itself that does all this. If I said it was me that was doing it, I'd be misleading you. It's this peace, this happiness working here through me, and through all of you, that is unchanging, never dying. This peace, this joy is what all your traditions and rituals point toward—this undying state, this eternal presence.

⁵⁵Yet ye have not known him; but I know him: and if I should say, I know him not, I shall be a liar like unto you: but I know him, and keep his saying.

⁵⁶Your father Abraham rejoiced to see my day: and he saw *it*, and was glad.

⁵⁷Then said the Jews unto him, Thou art not yet fifty years old, and hast thou seen Abraham?

⁵⁸Jesus said unto them, Verily, verily, I say unto you, Before Abraham was, I am.

⁵⁹Then took they up stones to cast at him: but Jesus hid himself, and went out of the temple, going through the midst of them, and so passed by.

55. "Although this joyful state or peaceable presence is what our traditions and rituals all point to, most of you have not yet incorporated this state, allowed this presence into your daily lives, your momentary experience. But this state is now my state and if I were to deny it, I would be a liar. Happiness, or peace is my daily experience and I am continually supported and led and moved by this ancient presence.

56. "I know that those who started our traditions, who first formed the rituals, would be pleased, delighted to see someone such as myself brave enough to incorporate the essence of the traditions and rituals into his daily life."

57. Again the elders of the tribe were somewhat offended. "You're still a very young man," they said. "And you are telling us that you have incorporated the essence of all our traditions and rituals into your daily life?"

58. "Happiness is not bound by time," Jesus said. "Peaceable awareness is what is present before the world began. I am that peaceable awareness."

59. This was the final straw for many of the people there. Jesus was claiming something that was just too much for them to understand, and too contrary to their traditions. They became angry and offended, and were ready to come after him with stones or whatever else they could lay their hands on. Curiously, though, Jesus was very calm, and peaceable. He simply walked through the crowd, out of the meeting hall, into the market, as if he were invisible.

Chapter 9

¹And as *Jesus* passed by, he saw a man which was blind from *his* birth.

²And his disciples asked him, saying, Master, who did sin, this man, or his parents, that he was born blind?

³Jesus answered, Neither hath this man sinned, nor his parents: but that the works of God should be made manifest in him.

⁴I must work the works of him that sent me, while it is day: the night cometh, when no man can work.

⁵As long as I am in the world, I am the light of the world.

⁶When he had thus spoken, he spat on the ground, and made clay of the spittle, and he anointed the eyes of the blind man with the clay,

⁷And said unto him, Go, wash in the pool of Siloam, (which is by interpretation, Sent.) He went his way therefore, and washed, and came seeing.

Chapter 9

1. In the market place, as Jesus was walking by he saw a man who had been blind since birth.

2. His friends who were with him asked, "Why was this fellow born this way? Was it because of something he did in one of his past lives or because of something his parents did or was it just because of the general condition of humanity that causes these things?"

3. Jesus said, "The happiness that is in everybody is always pure and untouched, timeless and perfect, regardless of any outer appearances. This man's apparent unhappiness is not his true condition. Nothing can diminish his essence including past lives or parental influences or the human condition. He, like all of us, is here simply to reveal the beauty and grace and dominion of happiness.

4. "Happiness continues to work through me, demonstrate itself though me, as I have been indicating to you all along. A time is coming when I will no longer be demonstrating like this, through this personal form.

5. "The happiness, the peace, the love that I demonstrate here now for you, through this human form, can be demonstrated through each of your own forms. This happiness, this peace is the eternal light of life itself."

6. After saying these things he reached down and picked up a bit of clay, then spit on the clay. Then he went to the blind man and gently rubbed a bit of the clay over each of the man's eyes.

7. After doing this, Jesus said, "Okay now go up to the pool there by the old spring and simply wash the clay away."

[8] The neighbours therefore, and they which before had seen him that he was blind, said, Is not this he that sat and begged?

[9] Some said, This is he: others *said*, He is like him: *but* he said, I am he.

[10] Therefore said they unto him, How were thine eyes opened?

[11] He answered and said, A man that is called Jesus made clay, and anointed mine eyes, and said unto me, Go to the pool of Siloam, and wash: and I went and washed, and I received sight.

[12] Then said they unto him, Where is he? He said, I know not.

[13] They brought to the Pharisees him that aforetime was blind.

[14] And it was the sabbath day when Jesus made the clay, and opened his eyes.

[15] Then again the Pharisees also asked him how he had received his sight. He said unto them, He put clay upon mine eyes, and I washed, and do see.

The blind man did this, and when he returned he was able to see the world for the first time in his life.

⁸. The people around him were of course quite familiar with this blind man. They saw him coming and were amazed. "Is this the same blind man who sat here for years and years begging on the corner?" they asked.

⁹· "No, it must be somebody just like him," others said, not able to believe it was the same fellow. "No, it is really me," the man who had been blind said, quite happily.

¹⁰. "How did this happen?" the people wanted to know. "What happened to your eyes?"

¹¹· He told them how a fellow named Jesus had simply put a little spittle on some mud, then washed the mud over his eyes. "He told me to go wash in the old spring pool. When I did, suddenly I could see."

¹². The people were obviously impressed. "Where is this man named Jesus?" they asked. "I don't know," the man replied.

¹³ So the people took the man who had been blind to the leaders of the tribe to show the leaders what had happened.

¹⁴. Again, tradition and ritual had designated this as a holy day, when people were not supposed to work or engage in any type of business.

¹⁵· Naturally, the elders asked the man what had happened and the man repeated his story, that Jesus had put clay on his eyes, told him to go to the pool and wash it off, which the man did, and when he washed it off he discovered he could see.

¹⁶Therefore said some of the Pharisees, This man is not of God, because he keepeth not the sabbath day. Others said, How can a man that is a sinner do such miracles? And there was a division among them.

¹⁷They say unto the blind man again, What sayest thou of him, that he hath opened thine eyes? He said, He is a prophet.

¹⁸But the Jews did not believe concerning him, that he had been blind, and received his sight, until they called the parents of him that had received his sight.

¹⁹And they asked them, saying, Is this your son, who ye say was born blind? how then doth he now see?

²⁰His parents answered them and said, We know that this is our son, and that he was born blind:

²¹But by what means he now seeth, we know not; or who hath opened his eyes, we know not: he is of age; ask him: he shall speak for himself.

²²These *words* spake his parents, because they feared the Jews: for the Jews had agreed already, that if any man did confess that he was Christ, he should be put out of the synagogue.

Chapter Nine: Happiness Opens Our Eyes

[16.] Again, the elders of the tribe began to bicker amongst themselves. Some of them wanted to simply ignore the miracle that had happened here. Others instead pointed out that Jesus again had snubbed tradition by doing these works on a holy day, which proved his unworthiness. Still others asked, "how can he be unworthy if he is able to perform such a feat as bringing sight to a blind man?"

[17.] So they asked the blind man himself, "What do you think about him? What's your opinion?" The man who had been blind replied, "Jesus exudes happiness. He is happiness. It's because of his happiness that I'm now able to see. His happiness is what I see, in him and in me."

[18.] Some of the tribe members still didn't believe him, and in fact, because there was such a glow about him, doubted that he was the same man who had been blind. They called for the man's parents to come to the meeting hall.

[19.] When the parents arrived, they asked them, "Is this your son, the one who has been blind from birth? And if so, how do you explain the fact that he now can see?"

[20.] His parents answered, "Yes, this our son, for sure. And for sure he was born blind, and has been blind all of his life.

[21.] "But we have no idea what happened. We can't tell you why or how he is now able to see, why he is no longer blind. We don't know who it was that did this for him. But even though he was blind, he is not ignorant or dumb, and he is quite able to speak for himself. So why don't you just ask him?"

[22.] The parents were a bit intimidated by the elders of the tribe. The elders had laid down so many rules and regulations, and were following so many rules and regulations from tradition, that it was very easy to offend them in some way or another, without even knowing it.

²³Therefore said his parents, He is of age; ask him.

²⁴Then again called they the man that was blind, and said unto him, Give God the praise: we know that this man is a sinner.

²⁵He answered and said, Whether he be a sinner *or no*, I know not: one thing I know, that, whereas I was blind, now I see.

²⁶Then said they to him again, What did he to thee? how opened he thine eyes?

²⁷He answered them, I have told you already, and ye did not hear: wherefore would ye hear *it* again? will ye also be his disciples?

²⁸Then they reviled him, and said, Thou art his disciple; but we are Moses' disciples.

²⁹We know that God spake unto Moses: *as for* this *fellow*, we know not from whence he is.

Chapter Nine: Happiness Opens Our Eyes   145

One of the harshest punishments anyone can suffer is banishment from the tribe, and this was what would happen to anyone who claimed to know the truth directly, without reliance or reference to tradition or ritual.

23. This was why the parents didn't want to claim to know or understand what had happened to their son, and encouraged the elders to ask him directly.

24. The elders called the man again to question him further. "Tell us how you were saved by a miracle directly from God," the elders said. "And tell us that Jesus didn't have anything to do with it, because we know that Jesus is just an unhappy troublemaker who dishonors and makes fun of our traditions and rituals."

25. The man who had been blind replied very calmly. "I don't know about these things. He may indeed be just an unhappy troublemaker. What I do know, though, without a doubt, is that before he came to me, before I met him, I was blind. And now I can see."

26. "Okay," the elders replied. "What exactly did he do to you? How did he make your eyes able to see?"

27. The man grew a little impatient with them. "I've told you already, several times, how it happened. If I tell you again, this time will you change your hearts and be Jesus' friends?"

28. The elders became angry at this impertinence. "It's clear that you already are one of his friends," they said. "But we are not. We follow the rules and regulations and traditions and rituals that have been laid down for us.

29. "We know that these are the things that have been proscribed for us to follow if we want to be happy. But we don't know anything about the type of supposed happiness that Jesus teaches, or where he got these notions

³⁰The man answered and said unto them, Why herein is a marvellous thing, that ye know not from whence he is, and *yet* he hath opened mine eyes.

³¹Now we know that God heareth not sinners: but if any man be a worshipper of God, and doeth his will, him he heareth.

³²Since the world began was it not heard that any man opened the eyes of one that was born blind.

³³If this man were not of God, he could do nothing.

³⁴They answered and said unto him, Thou wast altogether born in sins, and dost thou teach us? And they cast him out.

³⁵Jesus heard that they had cast him out; and when he had found him, he said unto him, Dost thou believe on the Son of God?

³⁶He answered and said, Who is he, Lord, that I might believe on him?

Chapter Nine: Happiness Opens Our Eyes

or why he thinks he has the authority to teach in the way he does."

30. The man who had been blind did not back down. "It's quite a wonder that you claim you don't know anything about the supposed happiness that he teaches, and that you don't believe he has the authority to teach in the way that he does. And yet here I am, a man whose eyes his happiness has opened, standing right before you, speaking with you plain.

31. "Unhappy troublemakers do not have power to make changes like this. Happiness itself has been working through this man Jesus, and happiness itself is what has caused my condition to now be what it is. It's not Jesus but happiness itself, peace, love, that moves in this way through him.

32. "How could it be otherwise? Has anybody ever before heard of someone who was born blind being made able to see?

33. "If it were not the real happiness working through Jesus, he would not be able to do anything close to this."

34. Still, the elders would not budge. "You've obviously been an unhappy person from the moment you were born," they said. "And now you are here telling us about happiness? Who do you think you are? Just get out, leave us alone." And so the security people led the man out of the meeting hall.

35. The word got back to Jesus that the elders had thrown the man out of the meeting hall, so Jesus went looking for him. When he found him, he asked, "Do you understand that it was happiness itself that healed you, that brought you sight? Do you understand that it is the happiness of the universe working through me and through you?"

³⁶He answered and said, Who is he, Lord, that I might believe on him?

³⁷And Jesus said unto him, Thou hast both seen him, and it is he that talketh with thee.

³⁸And he said, Lord, I believe. And he worshipped him.

³⁹And Jesus said, For judgment I am come into this world, that they which see not might see; and that they which see might be made blind.

⁴⁰And *some* of the Pharisees which were with him heard these words, and said unto him, Are we blind also?

⁴¹Jesus said unto them, If ye were blind, ye should have no sin: but now ye say, We see; therefore your sin remaineth.

Chapter 10

¹Verily, verily, I say unto you, He that entereth not by the door into the sheepfold, but climbeth up some other way, the same is a thief and a robber.

²But he that entereth in by the door is the shepherd of the sheep.

36. The man was still learning. "Exactly where is the happiness, my new friend? Who can point it out to me?"

37. Jesus smiled. "You are seeing happiness right now," he said. "And you are hearing it. Happiness itself is speaking to you in this very moment."

38. And then the man understood. "Yes, of course," he said. "I understand now. Happiness is right here, right now, everywhere, inside and out, always. Thank you. I understand."

39. And Jesus confirmed the man's words. "Yes, you do understand," he said. "Happiness itself has brought me here. Happiness has opened your eyes, and opens the eyes of those who can hear it. Sadly, when some people encounter this same happiness they feel offended and are therefore blinded, at least temporarily, to the simple grace being presented. It is those who cling blindly to tradition and ritual that are blind."

40. Some members of another tribe who were with Jesus at the time asked him, "Do you think we are also deaf and blind to what you are teaching here?"

41. Jesus replied, "Your own joy confirms whether you see or hear this teaching. If you cling to your unhappiness, you have not yet heard this teaching. If your unhappiness is lifting, you are hearing."

Chapter 10

1. Jesus said, "If your daily discipline and your daily priorities are not priorities and disciplines of joy, of love and peace, then you are, through your mistaken priorities, robbing humanity of its very essence.

2. "When you do make joy, love, peace your daily discipline, then through this discipline you are

³To him the porter openeth; and the sheep hear his voice: and he calleth his own sheep by name, and leadeth them out.

⁴And when he putteth forth his own sheep, he goeth before them, and the sheep follow him: for they know his voice.

⁵And a stranger will they not follow, but will flee from him: for they know not the voice of strangers.

⁶This parable spake Jesus unto them: but they understood not what things they were which he spake unto them.

⁷Then said Jesus unto them again, Verily, verily, I say unto you, I am the door of the sheep.

spontaneously blessing all humanity, and giving humanity a light, and an example in how to express our deepest nature.

3. "Although it is a universal calling, at its heart this remains a very personal work, a personal discipline that is most often shared through our private, personal relationships, in one to one encounters and small groups. Happiness itself will at times reach out through each of us personally to much wider numbers of people when the season is right and the reaching out is necessary. And yet at its heart, at its essence it is one human being touching with happiness the lives of other human beings through our simple, ordinary, daily encounters.

4. "And as our personal, peaceable, joyful discipline matures, our day lives increasingly exhibit the strength, the lightness, the artistry, the beauty and grace that others will come to trust, and lean on, depend on, and use to grow and mature in their own unfolding journeys.

5. "Our friends and family and associates will learn from our example the primacy and practicality of joy, of peace, and they will recognize it when they see it just as they will recognize the absence of true joy, deep peace, when it is not there. And in such recognition they will be led to walk the higher paths, engage the righteous work and follow leaders worth following."

6. Jesus shared these basic life principles with the people who were there, and yet many of them still did not grasp the simple lessons to which he was pointing, that the joy, the awareness for which they were searching through outer circumstances and relationships and conquests was already freely present within.

7. Jesus continued. "I am awareness. You are awareness. It is your old habits of clinging to your thoughts and feelings that blind you to this fact. The discipline I encourage is

⁸All that ever came before me are thieves and robbers: but the sheep did not hear them.

⁹I am the door: by me if any man enter in, he shall be saved, and shall go in and out, and find pasture.

¹⁰The thief cometh not, but for to steal, and to kill, and to destroy: I am come that they might have life, and that they might have *it* more abundantly.

¹¹I am the good shepherd: the good shepherd giveth his life for the sheep

Chapter Ten: Happiness is the Door

simply to let all your thoughts and feelings come and go and as they do simply rest in your own awareness, which is happiness itself. This discipline of resting in awareness, in happiness is the doorway into your own heart.

8. "Most of the traditional disciplines and rituals and teachings suggest you must do something different than what you are doing or go somewhere else or think according to some outside expert in order to find your happiness. These disciplines and rituals steal and numb your natural happiness. Your natural happiness is already here. You can enjoy your thoughts and feelings, whatever they may be, right now. What I say to you now you already know, because happiness is already your nature.

9. "Your happiness, or awareness is the door. I am that awareness in you. You are the awareness in me. We are each expressions of the same awareness, the same joy, the same love. We can go anywhere, be anywhere, think and feel what we ordinarily think and feel, and still remain with our happiness, our awareness. Happiness, which is awareness, is not limited by time or space, thoughts or feelings. It is always here with us. We are that happiness.

10. "If you were told you must do this or do that to be happy, to find peace, you were told a lie that robs you of your inheritance. At your core you are already happy, at peace. You were born happy, and born to be happy. Our traditions and rituals and handed-down ways of living have often misled us about the nature of happiness, and thus have often blinded us to our very being, our inherent nature. Let's have no more of that. I am here to remind you that life is rich, full and abundant in you right now, just as it is in me. Life itself is happiness. Life itself is peace, Life itself is abundance, and you are that life. I am that life. Let us no longer listen to those who would tell us otherwise.

11. "I am life itself, happiness itself, just as you are life itself, happiness itself. We are each here to express and expand

¹²But he that is an hireling, and not the shepherd, whose own the sheep are not, seeth the wolf coming, and leaveth the sheep, and fleeth: and the wolf catcheth them, and scattereth the sheep.

¹³The hireling fleeth, because he is an hireling, and careth not for the sheep.

¹⁴I am the good shepherd, and know my *sheep*, and am known of mine.

¹⁵As the Father knoweth me, even so know I the Father: and I lay down my life for the sheep.

¹⁶And other sheep I have, which are not of this fold: them also I must bring, and they shall hear my voice; and there shall be one fold, *and* one shepherd.

and enjoy the happiness, the love, the peace, that we are, that is already here in each of us. There is no other purpose for any of us here. This present joy is what we can safely dedicate our lives to.

12. "Unless you know and abide with the happiness that you naturally are, various circumstances will arise that would appear to take your happiness from you. Attending to your native happiness, your circumstances conform to happiness. Attending to your circumstances, neglecting happiness, your circumstances will splinter and unravel.

13. "We have been taught that if we have the right circumstances, we will be happy. I show you now that it is your happiness that creates the right circumstances. When you put your faith in circumstances, be they past, present or future circumstances, you have neglected the essence of your life.

14. "I am happy to show you these things. It is happiness itself, your own inner happiness, speaking and moving through me, that reveals these secrets of life to you. Your own inner happiness recognizes itself, and awakens to itself through these words.

15. "I have devoted my life, within and without, to this happiness. I am at ease with this happiness. I recognize happiness, peace, as my own nature. Happiness, peace, uses me as its own expression. What I am, you are too.

16. "We are all children of this same joy, this same peace, this same life. Regardless of the differing times or places or circumstances people experience across the earth, it is this same happiness that is working in them. Regardless of race, religion, politics, social standing or intellectual frameworks, it is this same happiness that is working in each of us.

[17] Therefore doth my Father love me, because I lay down my life, that I might take it again.

[18] No man taketh it from me, but I lay it down of myself. I have power to lay it down, and I have power to take it again. This commandment have I received of my Father.

[19] There was a division therefore again among the Jews for these sayings.

[20] And many of them said, He hath a devil, and is mad; why hear ye him?

[21] Others said, These are not the words of him that hath a devil. Can a devil open the eyes of the blind?

[22] And it was at Jerusalem the feast of the dedication, and it was winter.

[23] And Jesus walked in the temple in Solomon's porch.

[24] Then came the Jews round about him, and said unto him, How long dost thou make us to doubt? If thou be the Christ, tell us plainly.

Chapter Ten: Happiness is the Door

17. "This happiness that works through the wide variety of human experience, and in our own personal experience, appears to rise and then fall and then appears to rise again, fall again, rise again. In fact, though, the happiness itself, your own awareness is ever-present, ever still, radiant, available. The appearances, including our thoughts, feelings, sensations rise up and fall away. As we devote our attention to the unmoving awareness, we discover we are in fact this undisturbed peace, this happiness itself.

18. "Awareness itself is your undying, unending life. We spontaneously, abundantly share this life, this awareness with others not because we are commanded to but because it is our nature, our essence, and we simply have no fear that our awareness can ever be depleted or destroyed. "

19. Once again, Jesus' simple yet forceful words caused much commotion and some disagreement amongst those who were there listening.

20. "This unhappy man is crazy," some of the people said. "Why would anybody listen to such nonsense?"

21. Others disagreed. "Is this the teaching of an unhappy man, a crazy man," they asked. "Can an unhappy crazy man bring sight to a person who has been blind since birth? Isn't that proof of the truth of his teaching?"

22. Again, these things were taking place in the main city, after the harvest had been taken in.

23. Jesus went to the main meeting hall and then out to the large covered porch that was attached to the side of the meeting hall. This is where much of the official business of the community was conducted, and where people gathered to discuss the events of the day.

24. So the townspeople came to Jesus, and asked him, again, to be very clear about his mission. Was he trying to foment

²⁵Jesus answered them, I told you, and ye believed not: the works that I do in my Father's name, they bear witness of me.

²⁶But ye believe not, because ye are not of my sheep, as I said unto you.

²⁷My sheep hear my voice, and I know them, and they follow me:

²⁸And I give unto them eternal life; and they shall never perish, neither shall any *man* pluck them out of my hand.

²⁹My Father, which gave *them* me, is greater than all; and no *man* is able to pluck *them* out of my Father's hand.

³⁰I and *my* Father are one.

revolution? Did he want to be their king? Their priest? A community organizer? They wanted to know, exactly, what was his role going to be in their community?

25. Jesus said, "I don't know how I can make it more clear. You continue to resist what it is I am sharing with you. Happiness itself works through me, bringing peace, healing, harmony, abundance. This is the work and the role I bring to you. It is also your work, and your role.

26."Many of you resist this because of your long training in the rituals and traditions, basically the old way of thinking that would deny the immediate presence of joy, of love, of wholeness. You hope that joy or love will be the end result of your thinking and your activities rather than allowing joy and love to be the means. Many of you have identified yourselves with your thoughts and your traditions and rituals to such an extent that you can't hear the simple words, the simple teachings that I share with you.

27. "Others of you, thankfully, do indeed hear the simple wisdom of what I am saying, what I am sharing, and thereby recognize the joy, the life inside you as your ever-present guide and sustainer.

28. "You who can hear me and follow these teachings of joy will soon discover you have returned to your first, most natural identity, to that self, to that being that never dies. You discover that happiness, peace, awareness is your very essence and that it can never be taken from you by any person or circumstance or condition.

29. "Happiness, peace, awareness is the essence of all life, the origin of all life. We are brothers and sisters in this happiness, in this peace, and there is no one or no circumstance any where at any time who can separate us.

30. "We are joy. We are peace. We are one with each other, one with the life force, one with awareness itself."

³¹Then the Jews took up stones again to stone him.

³²Jesus answered them, Many good works have I shewed you from my Father; for which of those works do ye stone me?

³³The Jews answered him, saying, For a good work we stone thee not; but for blasphemy; and because that thou, being a man, makest thyself God.

³⁴Jesus answered them, Is it not written in your law, I said, Ye are gods?

³⁵If he called them gods, unto whom the word of God came, and the scripture cannot be broken;

³⁶Say ye of him, whom the Father hath sanctified, and sent into the world, Thou blasphemest; because I said, I am the Son of God?

³⁷If I do not the works of my Father, believe me not.

³¹· And again some people there thought Jesus' words were blasphemous, and many began to murmur and growl. Some moved toward him as if to do him harm.

³². Jesus said, "I have shown you the results of living as happiness. I have shown you healing, and harmony, and enrichment. Which of these things are you upset about?"

³³. The people who were upset with Jesus replied that they had nothing against the seeming miracles that were happening around him, but rather with his words, his claim that he, an ordinary man, was one with the essence of life, and that his happiness was somehow a divine happiness.

³⁴. Jesus took a deep breath and let it out slowly. "Don't our own traditions say that God is always with us?" he asked. "If divine happiness, divine peace is infinite, eternal, is there someplace that we can be that this happiness, this peace is not? Why would you have us cut ourselves off from our very roots, our very nature?

³⁵· "I'm simply pointing out to you what all of our spiritual traditions have also been pointing out—that the ancient peace, the unbroken happiness is our birthright, our inheritance. Regardless of your denials, this joyful inheritance is still a natural law working in each one of us.

³⁶. "Happiness itself moves me to say these things, do these things. The happiness that is in me is also in you. Are you suggesting that these words that happiness draws out of me, inspires me to speak, are blasphemous? I am happiness itself, peace itself. You are happiness itself, peace itself.

³⁷. "If something in you resonates with this observation, then you know what I am saying is true. If something in you does not resonate with my words, then let your eyes and ears see and hear what is happening here around me.

³⁸But if I do, though ye believe not me, believe the works: that ye may know, and believe, that the Father *is* in me, and I in him.

³⁹Therefore they sought again to take him: but he escaped out of their hand,

⁴⁰And went away again beyond Jordan into the place where John at first baptized; and there he abode.

⁴¹And many resorted unto him, and said, John did no miracle: but all things that John spake of this man were true.

⁴²And many believed on him there.

Chapter 11

¹Now a certain *man* was sick, *named* Lazarus, of Bethany, the town of Mary and her sister Martha.

²(It was *that* Mary which anointed the Lord with ointment, and wiped his feet with her hair, whose brother Lazarus was sick.)

38. "The blind see, the lame stand up and walk, the water is turned to wine, and multitudes have come to me in pain and have left without pain. This is how the ancient happiness, the unbroken peace works to show itself in our human affairs."

39. These words, suggesting that love, peace, harmony, joy are already functioning here in our ordinary lives, were still too strong and unprecedented for many of the people there. Again they became angry with him, and moved to take him and do him harm. But the happiness itself, the peace itself—that Jesus had been pointing to and making quite clear – now made Jesus seemingly untouchable. He simply walked away, through their midst, untouched.

40. Jesus kept walking, out of the city and over the hills with his friends to the river where John had first seen him and recognized the happiness that was radiating through him. Jesus and his friends stayed there in that river valley.

41. The friends and neighbors of John had heard John talk about happiness, but there had not been any of the happy healings occurring around John as they had around Jesus. Now they were saying that John was right about Jesus— that Jesus was happiness itself, and all the things that John had predicted about Jesus were coming true.

42, Jesus now was among many friends who knew him for what he was, and accepted his teachings in the way Jesus hoped they would be accepted.

Chapter 11

1. In a town where many of Jesus' friends were living a close friend of Jesus named Lazarus became deathly ill.

2. Lazarus was the brother of Mary, who had listened to Jesus and understood his message and had devoted herself completely to the joyful disciplines that he had shared. Her life had been completely transformed by his presence.

³Therefore his sisters sent unto him, saying, Lord, behold, he whom thou lovest is sick.

⁴When Jesus heard *that*, he said, This sickness is not unto death, but for the glory of God, that the Son of God might be glorified thereby.

⁵Now Jesus loved Martha, and her sister, and Lazarus.

⁶When he had heard therefore that he was sick, he abode two days still in the same place where he was.

⁷Then after that saith he to *his* disciples, Let us go into Judaea again.

⁸*His* disciples say unto him, Master, the Jews of late sought to stone thee; and goest thou thither again?

⁹Jesus answered, Are there not twelve hours in the day? If any man walk in the day, he stumbleth not, because he seeth the light of this world.

Chapter Eleven: In Joy, We Are Undying

3. So Mary and her sister sent word to Jesus, telling him about their brother's illness. Jesus himself had come to know Lazarus, and they had often enjoyed each other's company immensely. The sisters told Jesus that his good friend was dying.

4. When Jesus heard the news, he said, "Remember, there is no death. In our joy, we are all undying. Absolutely every circumstance unfolds for the purpose of demonstrating love, joy, peace, here on earth. We are all anointed to perform these demonstrations. This circumstance with Lazarus is no different than any other."

5. Jesus of course deeply loved and enjoyed and cared about Mary and her sister Martha and Lazarus, his old friend.

6. Nevertheless, when he received word of Lazarus' troubles, he didn't immediately get up and run to him but rather remained for several days right where he was, tending to the tasks and the people who were there with him.

7. After he had completed the work there he told his friends, "Okay, let's go into the city again."

8. His friends said, "We're not so sure you should do that. Remember how the people there were not happy with you. Some of them wanted to hurt you, even kill you ? Are you sure you want to go back there and see them again?"

9. Jesus smiled and shook his head. "Haven't I shown you already the power of joy, of peace and love when it comes from the inside? When we are at rest in peace, our outer circumstances conform to our inner experience. Knowing such joy, we can go anywhere on earth and be perfectly at ease.

¹⁰But if a man walk in the night, he stumbleth, because there is no light in him.

¹¹These things said he: and after that he saith unto them, Our friend Lazarus sleepeth; but I go, that I may awake him out of sleep.

¹²Then said his disciples, Lord, if he sleep, he shall do well.

¹³Howbeit Jesus spake of his death: but they thought that he had spoken of taking of rest in sleep.

¹⁴Then said Jesus unto them plainly, Lazarus is dead.

¹⁵And I am glad for your sakes that I was not there, to the intent ye may believe; nevertheless let us go unto him.

¹⁶Then said Thomas, which is called Didymus, unto his fellowdisciples, Let us also go, that we may die with him.

¹⁷Then when Jesus came, he found that he had *lain* in the grave four days already.

¹⁸Now Bethany was nigh unto Jerusalem, about fifteen furlongs off:

10. "If we don't know the inner joy, the inner peace, then we are not safe anywhere, even in our own homes, our own beds. Without the inner joy, we make ourselves vulnerable to every circumstance that comes along."

11. After sharing these insights, Jesus said, "Okay it's time. Our old buddy Lazarus is sleeping. Time to go wake him up."

12. Jesus' friends were a bit relieved, hearing Jesus say that Lazarus was only sleeping. If he was sleeping, that meant he might recuperate.

13. However, at the time Jesus knew that Lazarus' condition, at least according to human eyes, was not just sleeping.

14. Jesus recognized what his friends were hoping, so he spoke quite directly. "Lazarus' body has died," Jesus said.

15. "It was so arranged by happiness itself, peace itself, that I was not there at the time," he said. "I was not there because life still has wonderful demonstrations in store for all of us. Let's go see Lazarus."

16. His friends assumed that Jesus meant that he, too, was about to pass on. How else could he see Lazarus? So one of his close friends suggested to the others, "Let's go with him. If Jesus is going to die, we should die with him."

17. By the time they arrived at Lazarus' home town they found that Lazarus's body had indeed died, four days previously. So the body had been in the burial crypt for four days.

18. Lazarus' village was only a couple of miles outside of the main city where the tribe would gather at the meeting house.

¹⁹And many of the Jews came to Martha and Mary, to comfort them concerning their brother.

²⁰Then Martha, as soon as she heard that Jesus was coming, went and met him: but Mary sat *still* in the house.

²¹Then said Martha unto Jesus, Lord, if thou hadst been here, my brother had not died.

²²But I know, that even now, whatsoever thou wilt ask of God, God will give *it* thee.

²³Jesus saith unto her, Thy brother shall rise again.

²⁴Martha saith unto him, I know that he shall rise again in the resurrection at the last day.

²⁵Jesus said unto her, I am the resurrection, and the life: he that believeth in me, though he were dead, yet shall he live:

²⁶And whosoever liveth and believeth in me shall never die. Believest thou this?

Chapter Eleven: In Joy, We Are Undying

[19.] Therefore, when they heard of Lazarus' death, many of the tribe had come up to the village to comfort Mary and Martha, Lazarus' sisters, and see if there was anything they could do.

[20.] When they heard that Jesus and his friends were coming up the road, Martha quickly left the house and went out to greet them. Mary stayed back in the house.

[21.] When Martha met Jesus on the road, she told him, a little angry, "If you had come earlier, if you had been here, my brother would not have died."

[22.] Then she softened. "But I still have faith in you, and who you are. You are happiness and peace and bring this to everything you do. I know that because you understand joy and peace, whatever you want to happen, happens."

[23.] Jesus smiled at her. He knew what she was thinking, hoping, though she hadn't come right out and said it. "Your brother will be okay," Jesus said softly. "He'll come out of that grave they have him in."

[24.] Martha said, "Do you mean, in heaven? He'll be okay in heaven? That he'll leave the grave and go to heaven?"

[25.] Jesus said, "Heaven is here on earth right now, right where we are. Heaven is the essence of life, it is the joy, the peace that we have been talking about, that we have been demonstrating. It is within each of us. Regardless of our outer circumstances, no matter how dark they appear, if we recognize the light, the joy, the peace that is within, outer circumstances change to reflect the inner.

[26.] "Those who recognize this life essence, this joy within, and allow their lives to be devoted to this essence, to be infused with this essence, have discovered that presence which never dies. Do you understand this? Can you see this?"

²⁷She saith unto him, Yea, Lord: I believe that thou art the Christ, the Son of God, which should come into the world.

²⁸And when she had so said, she went her way, and called Mary her sister secretly, saying, The Master is come, and calleth for thee.

²⁹As soon as she heard *that*, she arose quickly, and came unto him.

³⁰Now Jesus was not yet come into the town, but was in that place where Martha met him.

³¹The Jews then which were with her in the house, and comforted her, when they saw Mary, that she rose up hastily and went out, followed her, saying, She goeth unto the grave to weep there.

³²Then when Mary was come where Jesus was, and saw him, she fell down at his feet, saying unto him, Lord, if thou hadst been here, my brother had not died.

³³When Jesus therefore saw her weeping, and the Jews also weeping which came with her, he groaned in the spirit, and was troubled,

³⁴And said, Where have ye laid him? They said unto him, Lord, come and see.

³⁵Jesus wept.

²⁷· Martha said, "Yes, of course. You yourself have shown all of us how the eternal joy, the infinite peace expresses itself here in our ordinary, daily lives. There can be no doubt."

²⁸. Saying this, she felt at peace again, she felt the joy to which Jesus had been pointing. She thanked him and returned home. At home, she pulled her sister aside and whispered to her, "Jesus wants to see you."

²⁹· Mary was glad to hear it. She quickly slipped away from the people there and headed out to see Jesus.

³⁰· Jesus and his friends were still on the outskirts of town, where Martha had been talking with him.

³¹. But the people back at the house, who had come to be with Mary and Martha and to console and comfort them about Lazarus' death, soon realized that Mary was leaving. They assumed she was going again to cry and be alone at Lazarus' grave, so they followed her.

³². Mary found Jesus where Martha said he would be. Mary went up to him, crying. She sat on a rock next to him, and put her head in her hands, crying. "If you had only been here earlier," she said, "I know Lazarus would not have died."

³³. The people who had been following Mary now also arrived. Jesus saw that many of them, too, were crying and all of them were in deep mourning for the passing of Lazarus. And Jesus felt their hurt, and, being human, spontaneously moaned and mourned with them, knowing them all and loving them deeply.

³⁴· Then he softly asked, "Where is he buried?" Quietly, they said, "Come, we'll show you."

³⁵. Because he felt their sweet humanness, Jesus cried.

³⁶Then said the Jews, Behold how he loved him!

³⁷And some of them said, Could not this man, which opened the eyes of the blind, have caused that even this man should not have died?

³⁸Jesus therefore again groaning in himself cometh to the grave. It was a cave, and a stone lay upon it.

³⁹Jesus said, Take ye away the stone. Martha, the sister of him that was dead, saith unto him, Lord, by this time he stinketh: for he hath been *dead* four days.

⁴⁰Jesus saith unto her, Said I not unto thee, that, if thou wouldest believe, thou shouldest see the glory of God?

⁴¹Then they took away the stone *from the place* where the dead was laid. And Jesus lifted up *his* eyes, and said, Father, I thank thee that thou hast heard me.

⁴²And I knew that thou hearest me always: but because of the people which stand by I said *it*, that they may believe that thou hast sent me.

Chapter Eleven: In Joy, We Are Undying

36. The people recognized again how deeply Jesus had loved Lazarus' company, and how much he loved Mary and Martha, and now how Jesus, too, was only human.

37. And some of the people wondered why Jesus had not come to heal his good friend. He had performed so many other miracles, and so many people in his company had received healing, including the man who had been blind from birth who had received sight. Obviously he had the power, so why had Jesus let his good friend die?

38. Jesus knew and felt what these people were thinking. His heart ached, and he could not help himself from moaning out loud as they approached Lazarus' grave, which was a cave with a stone in front of it.

39. "If you would, please, take the stone away," Jesus said. Martha, Lazarus's sister, objected. "It won't be pretty," she said. "Remember, he's already been in there for four days. There will be smells and who knows what else."

40. Jesus said, "Haven't I told you that the love, the peace, the joy that is in you is stronger than any outer circumstance? I've encouraged you to let go of your estimations of outer conditions and simply rest in the joy that is in you. As you do this, you will see the harmony, the grace, the wonder of this joy."

41. So then they took away the stone from the entrance to Lazarus' grave. Jesus turned his eyes away from the grave and took a deep breath. Finally, a smile came over his face. "Joy is right here, right now," he said, "just as it has been here from all eternity.

42. "This joy, this love is who we are, what we are. We don't need words to make it true. This love, this peace, this joy is always and already here present with us. Still, we use

these words to share with each other that inner truth, that inner reality that is common to everyone. We use these

⁴³And when he thus had spoken, he cried with a loud voice, Lazarus, come forth.

⁴⁴And he that was dead came forth, bound hand and foot with graveclothes: and his face was bound about with a napkin. Jesus saith unto them, Loose him, and let him go.

⁴⁵Then many of the Jews which came to Mary, and had seen the things which Jesus did, believed on him.

⁴⁶But some of them went their ways to the Pharisees, and told them what things Jesus had done.

⁴⁷Then gathered the chief priests and the Pharisees a council, and said, What do we? for this man doeth many miracles.

⁴⁸If we let him thus alone, all *men* will believe on him: and the Romans shall come and take away both our place and nation.

words so that we might recognize happiness itself as the reality we share."

⁴³. After reminding the people of these basic facts, he turned to Lazarus' tomb and called with a loud voice, "Lazarus, old friend, come out of there!"

⁴⁴· And in just a few moments, Lazarus appeared at the entrance of the grave. He was bound from head to toe in the wrappings that were traditionally used to wrap people after they had died. And his head was wrapped with the scarf that was traditionally tied around those who had died. Jesus smiled at his old friend, then turned to the people there. "Help the poor man out of those wrappings," he said. "Let him go free."

⁴⁵· Many of the people who had come to comfort Mary and Martha saw what had just happened. They realized that Jesus was pointing to something within everyone that is very powerful, very immediate, and literally life-saving.

⁴⁶. Still, this was something so out of the ordinary, so extraordinary that a few of the people still could not grasp what had just happened. These people went to the elders and rulers of the tribe and told them about the events that had taken place at Lazarus' tomb.

⁴⁷. The elders and rulers were dumbfounded. They gathered together to talk it over. "What can we do with this fellow?" they asked. "Miracles are happening around him all the time.

⁴⁸. "If we just let him continue to walk around and talk like this, before long everybody will be going to him. Everybody will be following him. Our traditions and rituals will be forgotten. The powers that be will wonder what we are up to, and they will probably come and take away everything we have worked so hard to accumulate."

⁴⁹And one of them, *named* Caiaphas, being the high priest that same year, said unto them, Ye know nothing at all,

⁵⁰Nor consider that it is expedient for us, that one man should die for the people, and that the whole nation perish not.

⁵¹And this spake he not of himself: but being high priest that year, he prophesied that Jesus should die for that nation;

⁵²And not for that nation only, but that also he should gather together in one the children of God that were scattered abroad.

⁵³Then from that day forth they took counsel together for to put him to death.

⁵⁴Jesus therefore walked no more openly among the Jews; but went thence unto a country near to the wilderness, into a city called Ephraim, and there continued with his disciples.

⁵⁵And the Jews' passover was nigh at hand: and many went out of the country up to Jerusalem before the passover, to purify themselves.

⁴⁹. Caiaphas, the man who had been elected leader of the tribe that year, became impatient with the people who were discussing this. "Nobody here grasps the seriousness of this. The potential trouble is actually much worse than what you're suggesting.

⁵⁰. "The powers that be could decide to kill the whole tribe, wipe us all out because of this man. Doesn't it seem right that just this one man should die to save the whole group rather than the whole group die to save one man?"

⁵¹. Because of his position as elected leader of the tribe, his words here were not just another opinion. His judgments were always given great authority by all the others, such that the people present now realized he had just predicted and given permission for Jesus to be put to death in order to save the whole tribe.

⁵². The tribe he was referring to was not only composed of just the people gathered together in that particular geographical area, but also of those who had spread out near and far across the globe.

⁵³. It was at this meeting that it was understood and agreed upon amongst the insiders that, because of their own fears and lack of self-understanding, Jesus would have to go, would have to die. So they began to plot various ways to bring this about.

⁵⁴. Such a decision, such a fearful reaction to his teaching amongst the insiders was not unknown to Jesus. It saddened him, but did not frighten him. Nevertheless, he left the main city and went up into a small village to the north in the mostly uninhabited hill country. His best friends, of course, went with him.

⁵⁵. Yet another of the tribe's traditional holy days with traditional rituals and feasting was approaching. Many people were leaving their country homes and going into

⁵⁶Then sought they for Jesus, and spake among themselves, as they stood in the temple, What think ye, that he will not come to the feast?

⁵⁷Now both the chief priests and the Pharisees had given a commandment, that, if any man knew where he were, he should shew *it*, that they might take him

Chapter 12

¹Then Jesus six days before the passover came to Bethany, where Lazarus was which had been dead, whom he raised from the dead.

²There they made him a supper; and Martha served: but Lazarus was one of them that sat at the table with him.

³Then took Mary a pound of ointment of spikenard, very costly, and anointed the feet of Jesus, and wiped his feet with her hair: and the house was filled with the odour of the ointment.

Chapter Twelve: The Time for Happiness Has Come

the main village in order to perform their rituals and be ready for the feasting holy day.

56. They were surprised that Jesus wasn't there. Gossip and rumors were spreading in the main meeting house about why he wasn't there. Some of the folks suggested that Jesus and his friends thought they were too good to be part of the traditional activities. Others, who knew him better, and had heard him teach, knew that something else must be happening.

57. The elders and leaders of the tribe were disappointed that Jesus had not shown up for the rituals. They issued an order that anybody who knew Jesus' whereabouts should contact them and let them know where Jesus was, because they intended to talk with him.

Chapter 12

1. A little less than week before the traditional rituals and feasts were to take place Jesus and his friends went back to the small town where he had called Lazarus up and out of the grave.

2. The friends decided they wanted to prepare a nice dinner for Jesus, which they did. They all came to the dinner, sitting down to one long table. Even Lazarus was there. Martha was the hostess, helping serve and making sure everything was as it should be.

3. At the dinner, Mary, Lazarus' sister, brought out an expensive alabaster jar which contained a large amount of muskroot, a very precious oil used as incense in the rituals and traditions in the meeting house. Mary took the oil and with her own hair wiped and massaged Jesus' feet with it. Doing this filled the whole room with a wonderful scent.

⁴Then saith one of his disciples, Judas Iscariot, Simon's *son*, which should betray him,

⁵Why was not this ointment sold for three hundred pence, and given to the poor?

⁶This he said, not that he cared for the poor; but because he was a thief, and had the bag, and bare what was put therein.

⁷Then said Jesus, Let her alone: against the day of my burying hath she kept this.

⁸For the poor always ye have with you; but me ye have not always.

⁹Much people of the Jews therefore knew that he was there: and they came not for Jesus' sake only, but that they might see Lazarus also, whom he had raised from the dead.

¹⁰But the chief priests consulted that they might put Lazarus also to death;

Chapter Twelve: The Time for Happiness Has Come

4. Judas was the treasurer of the group and knew how much this oil cost. He was one who had not yet recognized the depth of the work that Jesus was doing here, and therefore, for a little extra cash, was willing to spy on him for the elders and leaders of the tribe.

5. Judas said to Mary, "Why did you waste all this oil like this? You could have sold it and used the proceeds to help the poor. What you've just wasted here is a whole year's wages for some poor people."

6. Judas actually didn't care a whole lot about the poor people. Rather, as treasurer of the group, he was much more concerned with the cost of the oil and the money that was being wasted here.

7. Jesus said, "Oh hush up, Judas. I know that Mary was saving this oil to use in my own burial rites. It's better that she should use it here while I'm in the flesh with you, where we can all enjoy it.

8. "Poor people will always be with us, and we will always need to help them when and where we can. But this is a special night, and I won't always be with you like this in the flesh. So just enjoy, and be at peace here in this moment."

9. Word spread that Jesus and his friends were having dinner together. Many people from the village and surrounding countryside started to gather, not just to see Jesus but also because they wanted to see Lazarus, who had risen from the grave.

10. This, again, worried the elders and leaders of the tribe, who now realized they would not only need to have Jesus done away with but probably Lazarus, too, since he was proof of the power of Jesus' teaching.

¹¹Because that by reason of him many of the Jews went away, and believed on Jesus.

¹²On the next day much people that were come to the feast, when they heard that Jesus was coming to Jerusalem,

¹³Took branches of palm trees, and went forth to meet him, and cried, Hosanna: Blessed *is* the King of Israel that cometh in the name of the Lord.

¹⁴And Jesus, when he had found a young ass, sat thereon; as it is written,

¹⁵Fear not, daughter of Sion: behold, thy King cometh, sitting on an ass's colt.

¹⁶These things understood not his disciples at the first: but when Jesus was glorified, then remembered they that these things were written of him, and *that* they had done these things unto him.

Chapter Twelve: The Time for Happiness Has Come

[11.] The mere fact of Lazarus being up and walking around clearly demonstrated the power of joy, of life, and love that Jesus had been teaching. People could not help but see this proof, and understand and accept the powerful insights that Jesus had been sharing.

[12.] A crowd of people had come to the main city for the rituals and feasts. Word spread that Jesus and his friends would also be coming. By this time, everybody knew about the miracles that were happening around him.

[13.] Therefore, a large crowd went out to the edge of the city to meet him. Many of them ran ahead and swept the road in front of him, clearing the way, while others spread branches of palm leaves in front of him, to make his journey easier. This is the type of welcome and honor that was customarily shown to a king. "Here is the king of joy, the king of our happiness," they shouted. "He has come to rule over our land."

[14.] Jesus knew that this sentiment from the crowd was exactly what frightened the powers that be. He also knew that it was too late to do anything about it, and that the drama would have to play itself out. Accepting his part, he had one of his friends bring a young donkey that he could ride, thus fulfilling the scriptural prophecy.

[15.] The prophecy had said that the people would rejoice when the new king of the tribe finally appeared. He would bring freedom from all unhappiness. The people would recognize him because he would be riding a young donkey.

[16.] At the time, the friends around Jesus did not recognize what he was doing, or recognize the prophecy being fulfilled, nor did the people who had come to honor him in this way. Only later, after Jesus' final demonstration that happiness does not die, did it all fall into place and the

¹⁷The people therefore that was with him when he called Lazarus out of his grave, and raised him from the dead, bare record.

¹⁸For this cause the people also met him, for that they heard that he had done this miracle.

¹⁹The Pharisees therefore said among themselves, Perceive ye how ye prevail nothing? behold, the world is gone after him.

²⁰And there were certain Greeks among them that came up to worship at the feast:

²¹The same came therefore to Philip, which was of Bethsaida of Galilee, and desired him, saying, Sir, we would see Jesus.

²²Philip cometh and telleth Andrew: and again Andrew and Philip tell Jesus.

²³And Jesus answered them, saying, The hour is come, that the Son of man should be glorified.

²⁴Verily, verily, I say unto you, Except a corn of wheat fall into the ground and die, it abideth alone: but if it die, it bringeth forth much fruit.

Chapter Twelve: The Time for Happiness Has Come

people at last recognized what had happened, and what part they had spontaneously played in the drama.

17. Again, although Jesus had performed many miracles, it was the news that he had raised Lazarus from the grave that had spread to so many people and had finally convinced large numbers that Jesus' teaching was something new and powerful and true.

18. It was mostly these people, who had heard about this miracle, that were now coming to him and treating him like a king.

19. The leaders and elders of the tribe now saw without a doubt that things had gotten out of hand. It appeared as though nothing they could say or do would change people's high opinion of Jesus. Everybody seemed to love him.

20. Even strangers, who had come to the city from distant lands for the rituals and feasts, had heard about Jesus and wanted to meet him.

21. The strangers sought out Jesus' old friends and asked them if it was possible to arrange to meet him.

22. Jesus' friends talked amongst themselves and then went together to tell Jesus that strangers from distant lands were wanting to see him.

23. Jesus smiled and let out a deep breath. He, too, realized that his reputation had now taken on a life of its own. "The time has come," he said, "for happiness, peace to show itself fully in the world.

24. "Every expression of happiness has its time and place and natural rhythm," he said. "It's like the head of a stock of wheat. If it stayed where it is, and was not planted

[25] He that loveth his life shall lose it; and he that hateth his life in this world shall keep it unto life eternal.

[26] If any man serve me, let him follow me; and where I am, there shall also my servant be: if any man serve me, him will *my* Father honour.

[27] Now is my soul troubled; and what shall I say? Father, save me from this hour: but for this cause came I unto this hour.

[28] Father, glorify thy name. Then came there a voice from heaven, *saying*, I have both glorified *it*, and will glorify *it* again.

in the ground, then it remains a single thing; it is alone, and stays alone. Nothing comes of it. But when it is separated from its stock, and planted in the ground, then bushels of wheat eventually come from that single head.

25. "In the same way, if you assume your happiness depends on the separate people and circumstances and events of your current life, your experience of happiness is always going to fade away, because all forms rise and fall, everything always changes. However, if you recognize that your happiness, your peace is not dependent on separate people or circumstances or events of your life, your happiness will steadily deepen, your peace will steadily deepen, regardless of your outer conditions, even the falling away of your physical body.

26."What I am pointing to is the peace inside you, the joy inside you. If you want to follow me, follow the joy that is in you, the peace that is in you, which is love itself. That joy inside you is the essence of life itself. When you honor, give room and follow the joy inside you, you are honoring and making room for the essence of life. Life will then blossom in and around you.

27. "I recognize that the outer conditions that have now come together are taking me away. I am not frightened by these conditions, and will neither run from them nor fight them. I am still at peace. I am still happy. Outer conditions can not change this. This is what happiness itself, peace itself is now demonstrating here through me.

28. "Again, it is not my own virtue that is showing through here but rather happiness itself that does these things through me, peace itself that shows itself through me." After Jesus had said these things, and was quiet, the people there with him could suddenly feel, and hear and experience quite clearly within their own hearts and minds the peace and joy to which he had been pointing. They experienced how this peace had been there all along, just

²⁹The people therefore, that stood by, and heard *it*, said that it thundered: others said, An angel spake to him.

³⁰Jesus answered and said, This voice came not because of me, but for your sakes.

³¹Now is the judgment of this world: now shall the prince of this world be cast out.

³²And I, if I be lifted up from the earth, will draw all *men* unto me.

³³This he said, signifying what death he should die.

³⁴The people answered him, We have heard out of the law that Christ abideth for ever: and how sayest thou, The Son of man must be lifted up? who is this Son of man?

as Jesus had suggested, and would always be there. It was life itself. It was not dependent on outer expressions.

29. The people looked at each other and realized that everybody there was experiencing the same thing. The inner joy, the inner awareness, the inner peace that they all shared within was outwardly palpable. They were experiencing a presence, within and without, that transcended time and space, because the presence was not dependent on time or space.

30. "This is your happiness, speaking to you, from within," Jesus said. "I didn't create it; I didn't make it up. It is your own nature—our own nature--- speaking out.

31. "This happiness is the essence of life, and thus the rightful governor of all of our lives, of everybody's life. Unhappiness has no rightful place—either individually or collectively-- and spontaneously disappears as we recognize and follow our true authority.

32. "Happiness itself draws us to happiness," Jesus said. "The attraction to happiness is right, it is natural, it is graceful. I am that happiness. You are that happiness. This is our destiny. The forms of our happiness, even this form, come and go, but happiness itself remains."

33. He said this, knowing what was about to happen, pointing to the new life and the new understanding that would come about due to these events.

34. The people there didn't want to hear his words. "Our traditions say that the king of happiness, when he comes, will be here with us and lead us for all time," they said. "But now you say the forms come and go. Are you talking about your own form? Are you telling us you are leaving, after finally showing up?"

³⁵Then Jesus said unto them, Yet a little while is the light with you. Walk while ye have the light, lest darkness come upon you: for he that walketh in darkness knoweth not whither he goeth.

³⁶While ye have light, believe in the light, that ye may be the children of light. These things spake Jesus, and departed, and did hide himself from them.

³⁷But though he had done so many miracles before them, yet they believed not on him:

³⁸That the saying of Esaias the prophet might be fulfilled, which he spake, Lord, who hath believed our report? and to whom hath the arm of the Lord been revealed?

³⁹Therefore they could not believe, because that Esaias said again,

⁴⁰He hath blinded their eyes, and hardened their heart; that they should not see with *their* eyes, nor understand with *their* heart, and be converted, and I should heal them.

35. "I'm here now to point out the light inside you, which is your own awareness," Jesus said. "I'm pointing you to your peace, your love. This is the light inside you. Let this light guide you. If you look for guidance from the outside, you will be blind and not know where you are going and will therefore often stumble.

36. "It is your own inner joy that I am pointing you toward. Trust it, like a child trusts her parents. Trust your peace. Trust your love. Let it guide your way." He didn't know how he could make it any more plain. He smiled, waved, and walked away, disappearing over the hills, into the woods.

37. Jesus had shown the people the miraculous nature of their inner joy, how it consistently heals and prospers and harmonizes human experience. Still, there were many people who did not understand his teaching, who resisted it, blindly holding to their hope and faith that some outer ritual or tradition would some day make them whole.

38. Throughout human history men and women have appeared who have similarly recognized the joy, the peace, the power that comes from within, and time after time these individuals have met similar resistance from those around them. The ancient habit of relying on outer forms, of attaching attention and hope and faith to outer forms is a hard habit to outgrow.

39. The people around Jesus were shackled by this same ancient faith in their outer forms, traditions and rituals.

40. It is the habit of fixing attention on outer remedies that keeps people from experiencing the healing peace, the prospering joy that is already extant within. With attention fixed on outer remedies their inner eyes are blinded, their inner ears are made deaf, and most sadly, their love of life grows dry and withers because the inner wellsprings have been shut off.

⁴¹These things said Esaias, when he saw his glory, and spake of him.

⁴²Nevertheless among the chief rulers also many believed on him; but because of the Pharisees they did not confess *him*, lest they should be put out of the synagogue:

⁴³For they loved the praise of men more than the praise of God.

⁴⁴Jesus cried and said, He that believeth on me, believeth not on me, but on him that sent me.

⁴⁵And he that seeth me seeth him that sent me.

⁴⁶I am come a light into the world, that whosoever believeth on me should not abide in darkness.

⁴⁷And if any man hear my words, and believe not, I judge him not: for I came not to judge the world, but to save the world.

Chapter Twelve: The Time for Happiness Has Come

⁴¹. This is not a new observation. These are the same insights put forth by those who came before us, trying to lead us out of the darkness of ritualized ignorance into the light of flowing wisdom.

⁴². And there are those among us now, just as there has always been, who do in fact see the truth of these simple observations—that joy, love, peace reside always within. We always have among us those who are inspired by these insights and endeavor to live their lives by them. However, many of those who recognize the truth of these ancient insights do not speak up, for fear of making waves, or being rejected by the tribe.

⁴³.These are those who still mistakenly assume that their happiness depends on the good will and high estimation of others rather than on simple moment by moment connection with their own deeper inner reality.

⁴⁴. Jesus repeated his simple teaching. "The happiness, the peace that you see in me is the same happiness, peace, that is in yourselves. It is the same happiness, the same peace that is present throughout creation. This happiness, this peace, is the essence of all life.

⁴⁵ "What you see in me is what is present throughout all life.

⁴⁶. "I have come here simply to show you the light of your own happiness. It is already here, already there, inside you. All unhappiness dissolves in the presence of that light there inside you.

⁴⁷. "For some of you, what I say seems too simple, too straightforward, so you reject it. I understand why you do that. I do not hold your rejection against you. My only work is to teach and demonstrate happiness, and thereby to help remove all unhappiness.

⁴⁸He that rejecteth me, and receiveth not my words, hath one that judgeth him: the word that I have spoken, the same shall judge him in the last day.

⁴⁹For I have not spoken of myself; but the Father which sent me, he gave me a commandment, what I should say, and what I should speak.

⁵⁰And I know that his commandment is life everlasting: whatsoever I speak therefore, even as the Father said unto me, so I speak.

Chapter 13

¹Now before the feast of the passover, when Jesus knew that his hour was come that he should depart out of this world unto the Father, having loved his own which were in the world, he loved them unto the end.

²And supper being ended, the devil having now put into the heart of Judas Iscariot, Simon's *son*, to betray him;

48. "Happiness itself is here present for you, and in you. I can only point out that when you reject this happiness you shut yourselves off from your own wellsprings of grace. The unhappiness that you experience is not the result of some outer force wanting to do you harm. It is the result of your own shutting off of your inner light.

49. "Awareness, peace, love speaks through every form, shows itself through every form. What I tell you here is simply awareness speaking outwardly of its own inner wisdom. Listen to your own heart and see if my words do not resonate with the joy that is there. Your own heart confirms my words.

50. "This joy that you experience within when you hear me speak is the joy that never dies. Put your attention on that joy. Stay with that joy. It is what makes life worth living."

Chapter 13

1. Jesus was happy, and at peace, and he shared his happiness and peace with his friends and those who had been eager to learn what he had to share. Since he had dropped all identities except happiness itself, peace itself, which is timeless and formless, he could more clearly see the nature of the times and the particular forms around him and the events to which they were leading. Thus he was able to see that his own earthly work, his time in the flesh, was soon to be completed.

2. The dinner that his friends had fixed for him was over. Jesus knew that his friend Judas loved him but had still not learned the deeper lessons. Most particularly, he had not learned that the kingdom of heaven is within each of us. Jesus knew that Judas was still hoping that Jesus might get into politics and allow himself to be made king of the outer territory. Judas assumed that if he put Jesus into a position

³Jesus knowing that the Father had given all things into his hands, and that he was come from God, and went to God;

⁴He riseth from supper, and laid aside his garments; and took a towel, and girded himself.

⁵After that he poureth water into a bason, and began to wash the disciples' feet, and to wipe *them* with the towel wherewith he was girded.

⁶Then cometh he to Simon Peter: and Peter saith unto him, Lord, dost thou wash my feet?

⁷Jesus answered and said unto him, What I do thou knowest not now; but thou shalt know hereafter.

⁸Peter saith unto him, Thou shalt never wash my feet. Jesus answered him, If I wash thee not, thou hast no part with me.

⁹Simon Peter saith unto him, Lord, not my feet only, but also *my* hands and *my* head.

where he would have to show his power in the courts, then Jesus would be forced into accepting and demonstrating his rightful role as king. This was Judas' plot, based on this hope and his love for Jesus.

3. But Jesus knew he had nothing more to prove. He was already complete. Joy, peace and love were already the established powers that ruled the universe. Jesus was not politically ambitious.

4. Jesus stood from the table and casually removed the expensive robes his friends had given him. He was now wearing just a simple cloth around his waist. This is how the poor and the servants in the area mostly dressed.

5. Jesus then filled a bowl with water and took a cloth and began to wash the feet of his friends. This was the customary service at the time, generally performed by the servants and those of lower social order for those who had been traveling the dusty roads.

6. When he came to his friend Peter, Peter was very hesitant to let him do this. "I should be washing your feet," Peter said, "not you washing mine."

7. Jesus smiled. "My actions here are more telling than what you might now suspect," Jesus said. "You will understand better later. That will be soon enough."

8. Peter still balked. "No, really. I don't deserve to have you wash my feet. I won't let you," he said. Jesus said, "If you won't let me, that means you still don't understand me."

9. Peter understood now that Jesus was simply doing what love was prompting him to do, which is what he always did. Peter felt bad for his own resistance. "I'm sorry," Peter said. "Go ahead, please, wash my feet, and while you're at it, wash my hands and my head. I'm all yours."

¹⁰Jesus saith to him, He that is washed needeth not save to wash *his* feet, but is clean every whit: and ye are clean, but not all.

¹¹For he knew who should betray him; therefore said he, Ye are not all clean.

¹²So after he had washed their feet, and had taken his garments, and was set down again, he said unto them, Know ye what I have done to you?

¹³Ye call me Master and Lord: and ye say well; for *so* I am.

¹⁴If I then, *your* Lord and Master, have washed your feet; ye also ought to wash one another's feet.

¹⁵For I have given you an example, that ye should do as I have done to you.

¹⁶Verily, verily, I say unto you, The servant is not greater than his lord; neither he that is sent greater than he that sent him.

10. Jesus laughed and nodded. "Yes," he said. "You recognize what is happening here. The happiness, the peace, the joy that you are is always already whole and complete, already clean, pure, and not in need of washing. This outer action reflects the inner state. Most of you here recognize this, though not everyone."

11. And having said that, he glanced briefly, with deep compassion towards his friend Judas.

12. And then he finished washing all of their feet. He emptied the bowl, and hung up the wash rag and then put his own robes back on again. He sat back down at the dinner table. "Do you see what I've been doing here?" he asked.

13. "Over the months and years you've been with me you've seen that I have come to understand that I am not limited by time and space. Healing and harmony spontaneously appear around me because I have found and accepted my natural being, my original state of undivided awareness, which is peace, joy and love."

14. The friends there murmured in agreement that they had indeed seen these things. "If these wondrous things happen through and around me," Jesus said, "and yet still I am willing to act as your servant, washing your feet, then accept this as a demonstration of how you are to act toward each other, how you are to serve each other.

15. "Because we are each servants of the other, serving the joy, the peace, the love that everyone is, regardless of whether it shows outwardly or not. Let my example be your guide.

16. "Awareness is the great equalizer. The awareness that I am isnot greater than the awareness that you are. The awareness that made the universe is the awareness in each of us.

¹⁷If ye know these things, happy are ye if ye do them.

¹⁸I speak not of you all: I know whom I have chosen: but that the scripture may be fulfilled, He that eateth bread with me hath lifted up his heel against me.

¹⁹Now I tell you before it come, that, when it is come to pass, ye may believe that I am *he*.

²⁰Verily, verily, I say unto you, He that receiveth whomsoever I send receiveth me; and he that receiveth me receiveth him that sent me.

²¹When Jesus had thus said, he was troubled in spirit, and testified, and said, Verily, verily, I say unto you, that one of you shall betray me.

²²Then the disciples looked one on another, doubting of whom he spake.

17."Just knowing these things about the true nature of awareness, your own simple ordinary awareness, is your doorway to happiness.

18. "These things are very easy to understand, and very straightforward. And yet not everyone is ready to understand them or accept them for what they are. . Some of you here with me will continue to insist on the necessity of unhappiness, and thus bring unhappiness into your own lives and the lives of others.

19. "I'm pointing these things out to you now so that later, when various seemingly unhappy events come about, you will remember my words and know that I was teaching you the truth about the nature of both happiness and unhappiness.

20. "Let me say it again, though, so it will be very clear and immediate. Happiness is my very essence, my nature, just as it is your very essence, and your nature. Happiness is the light of awareness, the force of the universe. When you see me, you see happiness. When you see happiness, you see me. There is only one happiness, one awareness, and we all share this one essence. So wherever you find someone speaking of awareness, and living in happiness, I am there."

21. Such a joyous teaching seemed so clear, simple and obvious to Jesus, that he was saddened that not everyone would see it and accept it. He knew, for example, that Judas still assumed particular outer conditions had to be present before happiness was possible. "In spite of what I've just been teaching you," Jesus said, "One of you here still clings to the old beliefs, and therefore will soon bring violent unhappiness onto yourself and onto the rest of this group, myself included."

22. His friends looked around at each other wondering who it was to whom Jesus was referring.

²³Now there was leaning on Jesus' bosom one of his disciples, whom Jesus loved.

²⁴Simon Peter therefore beckoned to him, that he should ask who it should be of whom he spake.

²⁵He then lying on Jesus' breast saith unto him, Lord, who is it?

²⁶Jesus answered, He it is, to whom I shall give a sop, when I have dipped *it*. And when he had dipped the sop, he gave *it* to Judas Iscariot, *the son* of Simon.

²⁷And after the sop Satan entered into him. Then said Jesus unto him, That thou doest, do quickly.

²⁸Now no man at the table knew for what intent he spake this unto him.

²⁹For some *of them* thought, because Judas had the bag, that Jesus had said unto him, Buy *those things* that we have need of against the feast; or, that he should give something to the poor.

³⁰He then having received the sop went immediately out: and it was night.

Chapter Thirteen: Happiness Serves

[23]. This had been such a wonderful dinner, and everyone seemed to be getting along so well, and everybody seemed to be so close, that Jesus words seemed hard to accept. Simon Peter, one of Jesus' best friends, who had been leaning on Jesus shoulder with his arm around him, was very surprised.

[24]. "Who is it?" Simon Peter quietly asked, soft enough that the others would not here. . "Who are you referring to?

[25.] "Are you suggesting that one of us here is going to turn you in?"

[26.] Jesus gently shrugged his shoulders. He was breaking some bread at the time. "I've been feeding you all with these teachings," he said. "Who I feed next, you'll see, is the one who has not yet understood the depth of this work." And with that, he dipped the bread into his cup of wine and offered it down to his friend Judas.

[27]. Judas had been distracted, not paying attention, obviously disturbed, thinking about something else. But when Jesus offered him the bread Judas turned and accepted the bread. Jesus said, "I know you have an appointment to meet somebody. You best go ahead, go. Get the job done quickly."

[28.] The rest of the friends there with them at the dinner table were not aware of what was really going on here.

[29.] Since Judas was their treasurer, they assumed that Jesus was sending Judas to get their provisions for the upcoming celebration, or maybe to deliver more donations to the poor that they had been giving since so many people had been contributing to Jesus' work.

[30]. But Judas had a powerful sense that Jesus knew exactly what he was up to. Still chewing on the bread, and

³¹Therefore, when he was gone out, Jesus said, Now is the Son of man glorified, and God is glorified in him.

³²If God be glorified in him, God shall also glorify him in himself, and shall straightway glorify him.

³³Little children, yet a little while I am with you. Ye shall seek me: and as I said unto the Jews, Whither I go, ye cannot come; so now I say to you.

³⁴A new commandment I give unto you, That ye love one another; as I have loved you, that ye also love one another.

³⁵By this shall all *men* know that ye are my disciples, if ye have love one to another.

³⁶Simon Peter said unto him, Lord, whither goest thou? Jesus answered him, Whither I go, thou canst not follow me now; but thou shalt follow me afterwards.

Chapter Thirteen: Happiness Serves

following Jesus words, he excused himself and went out into the night.

[31.] After Judas had gone, Jesus said again to his friends, "The time has come to show that awareness has no end. The peace that is in us, the life, the joy that is in us, that is in the whole universe, can not be harmed. The time has come for me to demonstrate this for you.

[32.] "Yet it is not my personal demonstration, but rather the demonstration of awareness itself, life itself, that is making this demonstration through me.

[33.] "Good friends, my own personal, embodied expression of life will be with you for only a short while longer. You will look for me in this form but not be able to find me. This form, like all forms, comes and goes, rises up and falls away.

[34.] "But what I have taught you, what I have been demonstrating for you, is that we are more than our forms. We are in essence that undying joy, that eternal peace in which all forms rise up and fall away. So now I simply remind you again of what you already know in your hearts: it is your very nature to be happy, to be at peace. So be happy with yourselves, be at peace with yourselves, just at you are. It is your deepest truth. And when you honor your own truth, your own inner peace and joy you spontaneously find yourselves happy with each other, at peace with each other.

[35.] "People will know that you are my friends when they see that you are naturally happy, that you are naturally at peace, with yourselves and with all others."

[36.] Jesus was talking as if he was getting ready to leave, to go away. Simon Peter asked him, "Good friend, where are you going?" Jesus answered him saying, "My happiness is not going anywhere. But my physical form will be absent

[37] Peter said unto him, Lord, why cannot I follow thee now? I will lay down my life for thy sake.

[38] Jesus answered him, Wilt thou lay down thy life for my sake? Verily, verily, I say unto thee, The cock shall not crow, till thou hast denied me thrice.

Chapter 14

[1] Let not your heart be troubled: ye believe in God, believe also in me.

[2] In my Father's house are many mansions: if *it were* not *so*, I would have told you. I go to prepare a place for you.

[3] And if I go and prepare a place for you, I will come again, and receive you unto myself; that where I am, *there* ye may be also.

[4] And whither I go ye know, and the way ye know.

for a time, and you won't be able to see my physical form, or find my physical form. You are not able to completely follow me yet, or go where the physical form is going. But you are learning quickly. Soon you, too, will be able to demonstrate in your physical form what I am about to demonstrate."

[37.] Simon Peter disagreed. "I've been with you all along," Simon said. "I'll go wherever you are going. If you die, I'll die with you. I'd be happy to die in your place. Whatever comes, I won't leave you. I'm ready."

[38.] Jesus smiled, and gave Peter a big hug. "Thanks friend, but I know you're not ready yet. In fact, here tonight, before the sun rises tomorrow, before the rooster crows, you will find yourself in situations three different times where in order to save your own skin you will pretend not to know me."

Chapter 14

[1.] "There's never a need to indulge in unhappiness," Jesus suggested. "Awareness, or happiness is always already within you, it is you, no matter the outer circumstances. I too am awareness itself. So I am always with you.

[2.] "Awareness has many dimensions, many expressions, many subtleties. It's not just a single experience or a single feeling. Awareness has infinite potential for expressions. This potential is waiting for you, in you, as you.

[3.] "I have come here to show you some of the potential of the awareness that you are. As you turn to your happiness, to the peace within, you turn to me, and your potential will again be released in exactly appropriate ways and at the exactly appropriate times.

[4.] "The joy and peace that you are will always lead you, comfort you, uplift and support you no matter your outer

⁵Thomas saith unto him, Lord, we know not whither thou goest; and how can we know the way?

⁶Jesus saith unto him, I am the way, the truth, and the life: no man cometh unto the Father, but by me.

⁷If ye had known me, ye should have known my Father also: and from henceforth ye know him, and have seen him.

⁸Philip saith unto him, Lord, shew us the Father, and it sufficeth us.

⁹Jesus saith unto him, Have I been so long time with you, and yet hast thou not known me, Philip? he that hath seen me hath seen the Father; and how sayest thou *then*, Shew us the Father?

¹⁰Believest thou not that I am in the Father, and the Father in me? the words that I speak unto you I speak not of myself: but the Father that dwelleth in me, he doeth the works.

Chapter Fourteen: Awareness Is Always Present

circumstance. I am that joy. I am that peace. We are each that joy, that peace. "

5. One of Jesus' good friends asked him, "How will we follow our joy, our peace, if you aren't here to guide us?"

6. "I am happiness itself, which is awareness itself," Jesus said. "When you don't hold to the thoughts and feelings rising up in your awareness, but rather rest in awareness itself, you are close to me. When you are holding on to particular thoughts or feelings, or resisting them, ignoring the awareness in which they arise, you are forgetting me. To discover your life you must discover your joy, your awareness. There is no other way.

7. "If you now recognize your own simple awareness is joy itself, peace itself, you have recognized the depth of my teaching. This awareness is the background force, the background love of the universe itself. When you recognize that you are awareness itself , that you are joy itself, you recognize the universe swirling in you, as you."

8. Another friend said, "Okay, show us the happiness. Show us the awareness you are talking about so we can know what it is."

9. Again Jesus took a deep breath and sighed. "You've been with me through all these events, friend, heard all of my words of guidance," Jesus said. "And still you ask such a question. I'll say it again: you see me, you see happiness. You see me, you see awareness. Yet you yourself are happiness and awareness. Awareness see itself. This is who we are. This is what we are.

10. "This is what I've come to show you. Happiness is not far off. Peace is not far off. Awareness is not far off. This is our very being. The words I speak are words of peace. They come from joy. The harmonious happenings that you

¹¹Believe me that I *am* in the Father, and the Father in me: or else believe me for the very works' sake.

¹²Verily, verily, I say unto you, He that believeth on me, the works that I do shall he do also; and greater *works* than these shall he do; because I go unto my Father.

¹³And whatsoever ye shall ask in my name, that will I do, that the Father may be glorified in the Son.

¹⁴If ye shall ask any thing in my name, I will do *it*.

¹⁵If ye love me, keep my commandments.

¹⁶And I will pray the Father, and he shall give you another Comforter, that he may abide with you for ever;

Chapter Fourteen: Awareness Is Always Present

see in and around me do not arise because of my own personality but rather from joy itself, awareness itself."

11. "If you still have a hard time accepting my words, then simply remember the beautiful healings and enrichments that have happened in my company. These are the signs that my teaching reflects the laws of the universe.

12. "Again, it is not my own personality, my own powers that have brought these things about. It is the power of love, of peace and joy. As you rest in your own love, peace and joy, you will discover similar things happening in and around you. I've just touched the surface of the wonderful power of peace and love. You and those who follow you will see these same unfoldings, and more, much more than any of us dare to even dream about.

13. "Since awareness, which is joy and peace, is the original substance of the universe, there are no limitations on you when you rest in awareness. Anything you happen to conceive and believe, while resting in awareness, in joy and peace, is likely to come to you. And yet it is not these outer manifestations that you need, but the connection itself, the awareness itself, which is joy and peace. The manifestations are the signs of joy and peace, but not the necessity.

14. "Your joy is your power. Your peace is your power. I am that joy, that peace. I am happy to guide and support and nourish you through your own joy and peace.

15. "The best way to honor our friendship, and be true to yourself and to me, and to carry on the work that I have brought to you, is to stay in your love, stay in your joy, your peace. Recognize your awareness for what it is.

16. "Others will come after me who will help you more fully understand these words, and thus help you to be more at ease with my teachings, and to more directly demonstrate

¹⁷*Even* the Spirit of truth; whom the world cannot receive, because it seeth him not, neither knoweth him: but ye know him; for he dwelleth with you, and shall be in you.

¹⁸I will not leave you comfortless: I will come to you.

¹⁹Yet a little while, and the world seeth me no more; but ye see me: because I live, ye shall live also.

²⁰At that day ye shall know that I *am* in my Father, and ye in me, and I in you.

²¹He that hath my commandments, and keepeth them, he it is that loveth me: and he that loveth me shall be loved of my Father, and I will love him, and will manifest myself to him.

in your own lives the peace and joy that I am now sharing with you. You will discover that your sense of peace and joy continues to deepen and widen in your lives, relieving fear, sorrow and pain for yourselves and others.

17. "This joy, this awareness that is in you is mostly invisible to the world, and most of those in the world do not recognize the power and the grace that this joy conveys. And yet you are learning it, here, now, and what you learn will be with you always.

18. "The joy that I teach to you now will continue to grow. And after my physical appearance is gone others will come to help deepen and strengthen and broaden your joy. But even then, it is not the others that comfort you, but rather the joy, the peace that is within you that they are pointing to. This is our common ground, that will never go away.

19. "As I said, my physical appearance here is soon coming to an end. But the joy we share, the peace we share, I am that joy, that peace, just as you are that joy, that peace. This we will always have in common, and thus we will always be together.

20. "It's very simple and straightforward. Awareness, which is joy and peace, is the essence of life, all life, throughout the universe. As we rest in awareness, in that joy, that peace, we are free to travel the galaxies, and yet we never move. Through peace, through joy we are with each other, and in each other, and in life itself.

21. "As often as you can remember, let yourself become aware of awareness itself. Recognize that it is in awareness that all thoughts, feelings, sensations, relationships and circumstances are rising and falling. When you cease fighting the appearances in awareness and simply be with awareness itself, you are following my simple way; you are abiding with me, and I am abiding with you. Peace itself, joy itself is within each of us, and it is what brings us

²²Judas saith unto him, not Iscariot, Lord, how is it that thou wilt manifest thyself unto us, and not unto the world?

²³Jesus answered and said unto him, If a man love me, he will keep my words: and my Father will love him, and we will come unto him, and make our abode with him.

²⁴He that loveth me not keepeth not my sayings: and the word which ye hear is not mine, but the Father's which sent me.

²⁵These things have I spoken unto you, being *yet* present with you.

²⁶But the Comforter, *which is* the Holy Ghost, whom the Father will send in my name, he shall teach you all things, and bring all things to your remembrance, whatsoever I have said unto you.

²⁷Peace I leave with you, my peace I give unto you: not as the world giveth, give I unto you. Let not your heart be troubled, neither let it be afraid.

Chapter Fourteen: Awareness Is Always Present

together, as brothers and sisters, and even closer than brothers and sisters. We will always see and be with each other."

[22.]One of the friends there asked, "If you're going away, to a place you say the world can't see, how can we see and be with you?"

[23]. Jesus said, "You'll see me through your joy, your peace. You'll feel this joy and peace in your own inner thinking, and inner feeling and that is where we meet. Peace and joy are eternal, and infinite, and they work in your thinking and feeling in ways you are not able to fathom. Yet as it is happening, you will know, and recognize me there. I am in you. Life is in you. And we can never be separated.

[24]. "If you continue to look for your happiness and peace in the outer world, and trust the outer circumstances to bring you or keep you in peace and happiness, you have not yet understood my teachings. And yet these are not my teachings. They are the teachings of happiness itself, peace itself, awareness itself.

[25.] "I am happy to share these things with you while I am still here in the physical body.

[26.] "Awareness will send other teachers, other reminders of these things I am sharing with you. And they will help make these things even more clear, more real for you. And yet the spirit of happiness itself is what is always with you, always in you, and ever available to you for understanding, comfort and peace.

[27.] You can not have peace if you are not happy. And you can not be happy if you do not have peace. These are one in the same. It is your own inner awareness, this inner peace that I have come to remind you about. It is your own inner peace that I reawaken in you, and that will stay with you after my physical body has gone.

²⁸Ye have heard how I said unto you, I go away, and come *again* unto you. If ye loved me, ye would rejoice, because I said, I go unto the Father: for my Father is greater than I.

²⁹And now I have told you before it come to pass, that, when it is come to pass, ye might believe.

³⁰Hereafter I will not talk much with you: for the prince of this world cometh, and hath nothing in me.

³¹But that the world may know that I love the Father; and as the Father gave me commandment, even so I do. Arise, let us go hence.

Chapter 15

¹I am the true vine, and my Father is the husbandman.

²Every branch in me that beareth not fruit he taketh away: and every *branch* that beareth fruit, he purgeth it, that it may bring forth more fruit.

28. "I've told you that my physical body will soon no longer be available. If you understand the depths of what I have shared with you, this should not be troublesome. Indeed, when my physical body is gone we will be even closer, for I am happiness itself, and happiness itself, which includes your own ordinary happiness, is closer than my physical body could ever be. Happiness itself is what brings us together, and is greater than any of our personal expressions of happiness.

29. "I've told you that I won't be long in the physical body. And I've told you that my happiness and your happiness are the same happiness and that your awareness of this happiness will continue to grow and deepen and expand after my physical body has gone. I've shared this with you to show you how happiness is not confined by time and space, and that as we live in happiness, which is ever present, we are able to see both future and past unfoldings.

30. "From here on I won't be able to talk much more with you in depth like this about these matters. The ancient, ignorant momentum of unhappiness continues to demand attention. My very presence is a threat to such momentum.

31. "And yet my happiness is not diminished. I am not afraid. I am at peace. This is why I came here—to show how happiness, peace, has nothing to fear in the world. So let's go play our parts in this little drama about to unfold. Let's show the world how life can be lived through grace when we follow our joy, our peace, our love.

Chapter 15

1. "We are each expressions of the ancient peace, the ancient happiness from which the universe was born. This peace, this happiness nourishes. sustains and animates us.

2. "Whatever you do, or say or think that you do not enjoy, or that you are not at peace with, does not benefit you or

³Now ye are clean through the word which I have spoken unto you.

⁴Abide in me, and I in you. As the branch cannot bear fruit of itself, except it abide in the vine; no more can ye, except ye abide in me.

⁵I am the vine, ye *are* the branches: He that abideth in me, and I in him, the same bringeth forth much fruit: for without me ye can do nothing.

⁶If a man abide not in me, he is cast forth as a branch, and is withered; and men gather them, and cast *them* into the fire, and they are burned.

⁷If ye abide in me, and my words abide in you, ye shall ask what ye will, and it shall be done unto you.

⁸Herein is my Father glorified, that ye bear much fruit; so shall ye be my disciples.

others and leads only to unhappiness, stagnation and dead ends. However, when you allow your joy to inspire and guide your thoughts, words and deeds, then you bring rich rewards to yourself and others, and you are led to even greater joy, even deeper peace for yourself and others.

3. "These insights allow you to drop the heavy baggage of tradition and ritual and live free and clean here in the present.

4. "You are peace; you are joy. Rest in your own nature. If you try to do something without peace or joy, it is like a plant that tries to live and grow without soil or water.

5. "I have outlined for you the simple way of resting in awareness, which is itself peace, joy, love. If you follow this way, you will enjoy your life more, be more creative, more productive and you will thus be of great help to all those around you. If you don't rely on joy, you can't help.

6. "Those who continue to deny or ignore their native, inner joy are of little use to the greater community. By their own denial of this inner aware presence they marginalize themselves and are increasingly removed from partaking in the fruits of simple human relationship.

7. "Since awareness, which is joy and peace, is the first energy of the universe, when you rest in awareness you are unlimited and thus you spontaneously manifest in your experience whatever particular thing or person or relationship is appropriate, or necessary or beautiful in order to express the universal harmony.

8. "I want your lives to be full and rich and productive. This is what the joy we share brings about. It is in this joy that we have found our friendship, and based our friendship. Friends inspire friends to laugh and prosper and be at ease in the moment's fullness.

⁹As the Father hath loved me, so have I loved you: continue ye in my love.

¹⁰If ye keep my commandments, ye shall abide in my love; even as I have kept my Father's commandments, and abide in his love.

¹¹These things have I spoken unto you, that my joy might remain in you, and *that* your joy might be full.

¹²This is my commandment, That ye love one another, as I have loved you.

¹³Greater love hath no man than this, that a man lay down his life for his friends.

¹⁴Ye are my friends, if ye do whatsoever I command you.

¹⁵Henceforth I call you not servants; for the servant knoweth not what his lord doeth: but I have called you friends; for all things that I have heard of my Father I have made known unto you.

Chapter Fifteen: Friendship Thrives in Joy

9. "In the same way that I have discovered the root of my own being, and shared with you the peace, the joy that resides there, I encourage you now to stay with it and allow this joy and peace to continue to flow from you.

10. "The practices I have shared with you will keep you in peace, in joy. I encourage you to take up the practices and stay in joy, in peace, just as I do. From my own experience I can assure you these practice work.

11. "These things have I spoken unto to you, that my joy might remain in you, and that your joy might be full.

12. "Enjoy each other. Love each other, just as I have enjoyed you and loved you. We do this simply because it is the law of our being, the nature of our being, to love and enjoy each other, to be at peace with each other.

13. "To dedicate our lives to love, and joy and peace is the greatest gift we can give our family and friends. And there may come a time in our lives when it is better to give up our physical bodies than to give up the love, the joy, the peace that we know and share. To know that we would give up even the physical body before giving up the peace, or the joy that we share is the great bond that we friends have here between us.

14. "We become deep friends simply by following the natural laws of our own being, which are the laws of peace and love and joy.

15. "I have revealed everything I know to you about happiness and peace and love, and how to access it in your own life. I've shared enough with you now, and we've laughed and ate and drank enough together, and you have followed me and understood me, such that we no longer have the relationship of teacher and student, but rather, again, simply friends, deep friends, friends beyond space and time.

¹⁶Ye have not chosen me, but I have chosen you, and ordained you, that ye should go and bring forth fruit, and *that* your fruit should remain: that whatsoever ye shall ask of the Father in my name, he may give it you.

¹⁷These things I command you, that ye love one another.

¹⁸If the world hate you, ye know that it hated me before *it hated* you.

¹⁹If ye were of the world, the world would love his own: but because ye are not of the world, but I have chosen you out of the world, therefore the world hateth you.

²⁰Remember the word that I said unto you, The servant is not greater than his lord. If they have persecuted me, they will also persecute you; if they have kept my saying, they will keep yours also.

²¹But all these things will they do unto you for my name's sake, because they know not him that sent me.

16. "It is happiness itself that has brought us together like this. It is happiness itself that gives us both courage and authority to speak like this, and to share these insights with each other and with whomever else might be thirsty for such good news. It is happiness itself that allows us to grow and prosper and be healthy and wise and at peace throughout the entirety of our time here on earth.

17. "Again, such a happy life is not unnatural. It is the most natural life to live. Joy, peace, love is the law of life itself, so it is likewise the law of our own personal lives. Love yourselves, enjoy yourselves, and love and enjoy each other. This is how we fulfill the natural law.

18. "If the people around you tell you that this way of living is naïve, or impractical or unrealistic, even dangerous or blasphemous, remember they said the same thing to me.

19. "When you follow the old accepted tradition of struggling to find happiness and peace through changing your thoughts, your circumstances and relationships, the people around you understand this and will accept you for playing the game. When you begin to practice what I have shared with you, which is enjoying your peace and joy regardless of your thoughts or outer conditions or relationships, then the people around you may begin to distrust you and even actively work to block your way.

20. "We are in this together. My own experience here in the physical body, practicing the love and joy which I have found inside, has led to much misunderstanding and persecution. That may well be your own experience. And yet, there are those, such as yourselves, who quickly recognize the truth and power of this happy and simple way of life, and they will be inspired and led by your own example.

21. "Those who resist us and fight our way of living and demand we follow a different path than the one we are

²²If I had not come and spoken unto them, they had not had sin: but now they have no cloke for their sin.

²³He that hateth me hateth my Father also.

²⁴If I had not done among them the works which none other man did, they had not had sin: but now have they both seen and hated both me and my Father.

²⁵But *this cometh to pass*, that the word might be fulfilled that is written in their law, They hated me without a cause.

²⁶But when the Comforter is come, whom I will send unto you from the Father, *even* the Spirit of truth, which proceedeth from the Father, he shall testify of me:

following do so because they have allowed their thoughts and concepts to close them off from their own inner wellsprings, their natural state of happiness.

22. "We are learning to undo all unhappiness throughout the world. My teachings here have offered the steps by which this might be done. Many will hear these teachings and still cling to their unhappiness. It is understandable how people might have been caught in unhappiness prior to hearing these teachings. It is sad and embarrassing for people to insist on unhappiness even after seeing the works that happiness brings about and hearing the words of happiness so simply expressed.

23. "Happiness is the essence of life. To resist happiness is to resist life itself.

24. "I could not have made my teaching any more plain or simple than I have done. And the proof of my teaching has been demonstrated time and again in the healings and the harmonies that have been happening around me. What are people waiting for who still resist this teaching, and more importantly, this way of life? They cling to the dried twigs of their own concepts, of tradition and ritual while life itself is offering fresh bread and ripe fruit and fine wine.

25. "But I can not blame them for their rejection. I know that all things happen in their time. It was my time to bring this teaching here, and this demonstration, and it was their time to reject it. Our interactions here now will help others to see and understand the laws of life more clearly, and be more willing to return to their own peace, their own joy, because of the drama that is being played out here now.

26. "Happiness will send others to continue this teaching, just as it sent me. Life itself demands that the joy, the peace, the love that is the essence of life will be known and felt and relied upon by every human being.

²⁷And ye also shall bear witness, because ye have been with me from the beginning.

Chapter 16

¹These things have I spoken unto you, that ye should not be offended.

²They shall put you out of the synagogues: yea, the time cometh, that whosoever killeth you will think that he doeth God service.

³And these things will they do unto you, because they have not known the Father, nor me.

⁴But these things have I told you, that when the time shall come, ye may remember that I told you of them. And these things I said not unto you at the beginning, because I was with you.

⁵But now I go my way to him that sent me; and none of you asketh me, Whither goest thou?

²⁷· "You, yourselves, are expressions of this life, this joy, this peace and love. You have heard my teaching and seen my way of life and you are able to carry on what I have shared with you. It is happiness itself that carries on through you. I am that happiness.

Chapter 16

¹· "I have shared these teachings with you, and these demonstrations," Jesus continued, "so that you might better understand your own nature, and be happy, and at peace, no matter your circumstance.

²· "However, the momentum of human unhappiness has built up over many generations, so don't be surprised if you run into violent resistance and opposition for living your lives according to this teaching and practice. At times, you will be ostracized, and there will be those who assume they would do both the community and the communal tradition a favor if they actively oppress you and your ways, and even violently remove you if necessary from the scene.

³· "Have compassion for these folks. They do not yet recognize their own inner joy, their inner peace, and thus neither recognize nor find joy or peace in the wider world.

⁴· "When you experience this opposition and violent antagonism toward your simple discipline of peace and joy, you can remember what I'm telling you here. I didn't need to warn you about this in the beginning of our work together, because at that time my physical presence was sufficient to help you understand and practice this peace, no matter the outer circumstance.

⁵· "Now, however, my physical presence will soon no longer be with you. I return to objectless awareness, to peace, love and joy. You now understand what I am talking about, what I am pointing to.

⁶But because I have said these things unto you, sorrow hath filled your heart.

⁷Nevertheless I tell you the truth; It is expedient for you that I go away: for if I go not away, the Comforter will not come unto you; but if I depart, I will send him unto you.

⁸And when he is come, he will reprove the world of sin, and of righteousness, and of judgment:

⁹Of sin, because they believe not on me;

¹⁰Of righteousness, because I go to my Father, and ye see me no more;

¹¹Of judgment, because the prince of this world is judged.

¹²I have yet many things to say unto you, but ye cannot bear them now.

6. "It is clear to me, however, that you are sad and worried and becoming upset because I have just told you that my physical body will no longer be with you,

7. "This is all part of the learning process, the maturing process. You are still relying on my physical presence for your experience of happiness and peace. When my physical presence is no longer available, you will experience joy and peace in its more subtle forms, arising from within, ever available as your own awareness. After my physical presence has gone, others will appear who will point you to this same awareness, joy and peace, and yet even if they didn't appear, peace would rise up in you, call to you, and you will know even more clearly the essence of your own being.

8. "Happiness can not be stopped. It is life itself unfolding. The long momentum of unhappiness, however, can be stopped, can be brought to an end. And ignorance of happiness can be removed. The wisdom of peace can reign. This is the law of life, unfolding.

9. "People will awaken to the inner presence of peace and joy because in fact peace and joy are more real, more stable, more natural than unhappiness.

10. "True happiness is the not result of stimulating the senses. It is not the result of anything. It is an aware presence that was here before the earth was made.

11. "The unhappiness that has been ruler of our communities for so long is an imposter, an unnecessary attachment. We no longer need give our allegiance to such an imposter.

12. "Joy, peace and love will continue to teach you many lessons, and show you many wonderful things. Practice the discipline of releasing your thoughts, being at peace with yourself just as you are. Do this and each new

¹³Howbeit when he, the Spirit of truth, is come, he will guide you into all truth: for he shall not speak of himself; but whatsoever he shall hear, *that* shall he speak: and he will shew you things to come.

¹⁴He shall glorify me: for he shall receive of mine, and shall shew *it* unto you.

¹⁵All things that the Father hath are mine: therefore said I, that he shall take of mine, and shall shew *it* unto you.

¹⁶A little while, and ye shall not see me: and again, a little while, and ye shall see me, because I go to the Father.

¹⁷Then said *some* of his disciples among themselves, What is this that he saith unto us, A little while, and ye shall not see me: and again, a little while, and ye shall see me: and, Because I go to the Father?

¹⁸They said therefore, What is this that he saith, A little while? we cannot tell what he saith.

lesson you need or demonstration will gracefully appear in its own right time, at its own right place.

¹³. "Awareness itself is universal. Peace is without boundaries of time or space. When you rest in awareness, listen for peace, you are listening for the wisdom of life itself. Awareness reveals to you here in the present what you need to know of both the past and the future.

¹⁴. "We are in this together. Those who in the future teach you about happiness and peace teach you about me, just as I am now teaching you about those who will come after me who will teach this way of life. It is happiness itself, peace itself, awareness itself that we celebrate.

¹⁵. "Our love, our joy, our peace, this awareness is what brings us together and what we share as friends. I have been teaching this and demonstrating this from the beginning. Now it is your turn, and others in their time will likewise have their part in this joyful work. I am always present whenever joy and peace are being expressed.

¹⁶. "Even though my physical presence will not be with you much longer, we will always be together in this work, in this joy and peace. And it won't be long until we are all together again on the subtle planes in ways that are even more immediate and tantalizing than being here together in our physical bodies."

¹⁷. When Jesus' friends heard him talking again about not being with them much longer in the physical body, and that all of them would be together again on the subtle planes, they talked and murmured amongst themselves, wondering what he could mean.

¹⁸. Jesus' friends wondered if Jesus meant he was soon going to die, or just go away, or maybe disappear into the sky. They didn't know what he meant.

[19] Now Jesus knew that they were desirous to ask him, and said unto them, Do ye enquire among yourselves of that I said, A little while, and ye shall not see me: and again, a little while, and ye shall see me?

[20] Verily, verily, I say unto you, That ye shall weep and lament, but the world shall rejoice: and ye shall be sorrowful, but your sorrow shall be turned into joy.

[21] A woman when she is in travail hath sorrow, because her hour is come: but as soon as she is delivered of the child, she remembereth no more the anguish, for joy that a man is born into the world.

[22] And ye now therefore have sorrow: but I will see you again, and your heart shall rejoice, and your joy no man taketh from you.

[23] And in that day ye shall ask me nothing. Verily, verily, I say unto you, Whatsoever ye shall ask the Father in my name, he will give *it* you.

[24] Hitherto have ye asked nothing in my name: ask, and ye shall receive, that your joy may be full.

19. Jesus, of course, was not unaware of their concern and confusion. He smiled. "Joy is always present with you," he repeated. "Peace is always present with you. You wonder about our personal relationship, how it can be expressed first here in the physical world and then later in the subtle planes.

20. "Here in the physical world you will soon discover yourselves experiencing mourning, sorrow and regret while many of those around you are glad for the events unfolding. But your mourning, sorrow and regret will quickly turn back into rejoicing and understanding.

21. "It is like a woman while giving birth first experiences pain and discomfort and uncertainty, and then after the baby is born, she is happy and relaxed and grateful for the new baby.

22. "In the same way, in this brief season you will experience fear, anxiety and disappointment because of my leaving you but soon the deep reality of the nature of awareness, its peace and joy will come clear to you and you will never again lose your sense of its presence.

23. "You won't be dependent on my physical presence any longer. Your own inner sense of the ancient presence of peace and joy will spontaneously manifest in and around you everything that is necessary for a full, rich and beautiful life, on all levels.

24. "The universal awareness, or peace that we share is always complete, right here, right now. Before I came you had not fully recognized the power and grace and beauty of that peace. Now, as you turn to and rest in the uncaused awareness, anything in the world that you might have need of for your own expression of joy will inevitably come your way in its own right time and place.

²⁵These things have I spoken unto you in proverbs: but the time cometh, when I shall no more speak unto you in proverbs, but I shall shew you plainly of the Father.

²⁶At that day ye shall ask in my name: and I say not unto you, that I will pray the Father for you:

²⁷For the Father himself loveth you, because ye have loved me, and have believed that I came out from God.

²⁸I came forth from the Father, and am come into the world: again, I leave the world, and go to the Father.

²⁹His disciples said unto him, Lo, now speakest thou plainly, and speakest no proverb.

³⁰Now are we sure that thou knowest all things, and needest not that any man should ask thee: by this we believe that thou camest forth from God.

³¹Jesus answered them, Do ye now believe?

³²Behold, the hour cometh, yea, is now come, that ye shall be scattered, every man to his own, and shall leave me alone: and yet I am not alone, because the Father is with me.

25. "I have been sharing these principles with you as clearly and simply and openly as I am able. I am confident that the power and practicality of the discipline I have encouraged you to take up will continue to show itself to be increasingly useful in your lives.

26. "The discipline of releasing your thoughts, being at peace with yourself just as you are leads to a sustained consciousness of joy, a sustained consciousness of peace, and it is this consciousness that unfolds the graceful life in and around you.

27. "The fundamental nature of joy and peace requires that it work through you, manifest through you. This is the simple demonstration I have shared with you, and the lesson you have learned from me. I have shown you how joy and peace unfold, and you, my friends, have accepted me and my words and my works. This acceptance in itself begins the same unfolding process in you.

28. "My physical presence comes and goes. But the joy that I teach, the peace that I point to, is ever-present awareness."

29. His friends said, "Yes, thank you. Your words are very clear and simple and to the point.

30. "We have experienced joy and peace in your presence. And you have shown us how this same joy and peace is always available within ourselves as our own awareness. You have clearly demonstrated the transforming power of this joy and peace, and how it transcends both time and space. You have made it very clear to us. Thank you."

31. Jesus responded, "Yes, now you see, now you understand what it is I have come to share with you.

32. "However, events are now unfolding such that this small gathering of friends will soon be broken up. You will each need to take up the practice mostly on your own, and

[33] These things I have spoken unto you, that in me ye might have peace. In the world ye shall have tribulation: but be of good cheer; I have overcome the world.

Chapter 17

[1] These words spake Jesus, and lifted up his eyes to heaven, and said, Father, the hour is come; glorify thy Son, that thy Son also may glorify thee:

[2] As thou hast given him power over all flesh, that he should give eternal life to as many as thou hast given him.

[3] And this is life eternal, that they might know thee the only true God, and Jesus Christ, whom thou hast sent.

[4] I have glorified thee on the earth: I have finished the work which thou gavest me to do.

in private. I will not have you here with me. Nevertheless, I will have joy, I will have peace, and so I will have you and I will have the ancient aware presence that never wavers.

33. "As friends we have shared enough together that the inner joy and peace that I have been pointing to should now always be clear and available to you. Although our outer circumstances are about to become very tumultuous, and seemingly chaotic and unreasonable, rest in the understanding that the joy and peace that you now know can not be touched by these outer events."

Chapter 17

1. Again Jesus looked around and smiled at his friends and let out a deep breath. He closed his eyes. "Let happiness express itself through us and magnify itself in the world," he said. "Let peace express itself through us, and magnify itself in all that we do, and in everywhere we go, and in all that we say and think.

2. "Let us recognize this peace and joy as more real, more immediate than even our physical bodies. We realize now and accept that the ancient peace, the ancient joy never dies. Our bond goes beyond the rising and falling away of our physical bodies.

3. "We see that to live and move and have our being in this undying peace, this joy, this awareness, is the most natural way for us to live and move. Knowing such peace, such love, we never die.

4. "I have taught and demonstrated the graceful power of awareness, of joy and peace to my friends and to anyone who would listen. The work of this physical body is now complete.

⁵And now, O Father, glorify thou me with thine own self with the glory which I had with thee before the world was.

⁶I have manifested thy name unto the men which thou gavest me out of the world: thine they were, and thou gavest them me; and they have kept thy word.

⁷Now they have known that all things whatsoever thou hast given me are of thee.

⁸For I have given unto them the words which thou gavest me; and they have received *them*, and have known surely that I came out from thee, and they have believed that thou didst send me.

⁹I pray for them: I pray not for the world, but for them which thou hast given me; for they are thine.

¹⁰And all mine are thine, and thine are mine; and I am glorified in them.

¹¹And now I am no more in the world, but these are in the world, and I come to thee. Holy Father, keep through thine own name those whom thou hast given me, that they may be one, as we *are*.

Chapter Seventeen: Peace Magnifies Itself

5. "The natural, universal happiness of simple awareness is again known, honored and practiced here on earth. The joy that was before the beginning of time is active right now in our momentary awareness.

6. "These friends have heard my words and seen my works and have taken up in their own lives the discipline of joy, the discipline of peace. It was joy itself, peace itself that spoke to them from within their own hearts that allowed them to recognize the power of this simple way of life. It is joy itself, peace itself that has brought these friends together like this.

7. "It is joy expressing itself, awareness expressing itself that we now recognize as the power that is animating our lives, our world and the universe.

8. "It is joy that has spoken through me, and joy that has brought about the healings and the harmonies and the blessings that people have experienced. My friends here now recognize that it is not me but rather the joy working through me, the peace working through me that has manifested these things.

9. "I recognize and affirm that the joy and peace that flows through me also flows through these friends, and anyone who hears my words and understands and practices this way. I am with them, they are with me; we are united in our love and gratitude and joy.

10. ""It is happiness itself that brings us together like this. We belong to joy. We are the children of joy, of peace; we are brothers and sisters in this ancient family.

11. "My physical body will soon no longer be in this world, yet these friends, these brothers and sisters will continue where I have left off. Awareness itself never leaves. Awareness itself will keep these brothers and sisters in happy communion with each other and with the ancient

¹²While I was with them in the world, I kept them in thy name: those that thou gavest me I have kept, and none of them is lost, but the son of perdition; that the scripture might be fulfilled.

¹³And now come I to thee; and these things I speak in the world, that they might have my joy fulfilled in themselves.

¹⁴I have given them thy word; and the world hath hated them, because they are not of the world, even as I am not of the world.

¹⁵I pray not that thou shouldest take them out of the world, but that thou shouldest keep them from the evil.

¹⁶They are not of the world, even as I am not of the world.

¹⁷Sanctify them through thy truth: thy word is truth.

peaceable presence. The peace in one heart is the exact same peace in the other's heart. Through peace, through joy, this awareness, we are one being.

12. "We have all learned the lessons of joy, and the stories that we have lived out together here are the stories necessary for the unfolding of joy on earth, through us and through all those who come after us. Even our misguided lost friend, who has secretly gone to our tribal authorities to betray our trust, is a necessary part of our story. His betrayal can not diminish the fullness of joy itself.

13. "Again, I can not say it more clearly: my work here is to uncover and magnify the joy, the peace that is awareness alive in the human heart. We are happiness itself, peace itself, awareness itself. This is our first nature.

14. "I share these teachings, and give these demonstrations, and yet unawareness in all of its forms still claims much authority in the world. My teachings and demonstrations are direct challenges to such authority, so there is still much resistance to the work my friends and I are doing here because we are not swayed by the false authority of unawareness, which is unhappiness itself.

15. "Our work, our play and our lives take place here in the world. This is as it should be. We are not trying to escape the world. And yet with this teaching we no longer need bow to the false authority of unhappiness.

16. "Attending to joy, to peace, to awareness, my friends move through the world with natural grace, spontaneously expressing love, beauty and abundance, just as I have done.

17. "We are confirmed in this simple yet profound way of life by the immediate increase in joy and peace that we experience, and that those around us experience in our company. Happiness, peace, awareness is its own reward.

¹⁸As thou hast sent me into the world, even so have I also sent them into the world.

¹⁹And for their sakes I sanctify myself, that they also might be sanctified through the truth.

²⁰Neither pray I for these alone, but for them also which shall believe on me through their word;

²¹That they all may be one; as thou, Father, *art* in me, and I in thee, that they also may be one in us: that the world may believe that thou hast sent me.

²²And the glory which thou gavest me I have given them; that they may be one, even as we are one:

²³I in them, and thou in me, that they may be made perfect in one; and that the world may know that thou hast sent me, and hast loved them, as thou hast loved me.

²⁴Father, I will that they also, whom thou hast given me, be with me where I am; that they may behold my glory, which thou hast given me: for thou lovedst me before the foundation of the world.

¹⁸· "I have made this demonstration of happiness and peace here in the middle of our ordinary daily lives and now my friends are empowered by their own joy to likewise make this same demonstration.

¹⁹. "I have abandoned every identity that would rise up in me except the identification with the ancient peace, the universal joy, so that my friends can see that it is possible to live in the world in this manner and do as I have done.

²⁰. "And my friends here shall go into the world and likewise offer demonstrations of peace and joy, and others will discover their own true nature through these friends who carry the light.

²¹. "The happiness that is at the center of this work is a single, universal happiness. It is the ancient awareness that was here before the beginning of time, and that will be here after the worlds have ended. We are each expressions of this universal awareness, happiness, and in this universal happiness we have no division among us.

²². "We are one joyful heart, beating in infinite variety; one peaceful mind, expressing itself in uncountable ways; one beautiful body, dancing in unending rhythms. Neither time nor space separate us. Awareness itself is the maker and sustainer of this condition.

²³. "Joyful awareness is alive, and intelligent and loving, and it is working in each of us, unfolding our lives in ever more graceful and beautiful expressions. Through our own acceptance and practice of these simple teachings others are led to likewise recognize their own inner nature and find the joyful awareness that is the seed of their own being.

²⁴· "All forms rise and fall away, including the forms of our own bodies. And yet our joy, our peace, being formless, timeless, is indivisible, is undying and ever available.

²⁵O righteous Father, the world hath not known thee: but I have known thee, and these have known that thou hast sent me.

²⁶And I have declared unto them thy name, and will declare *it*: that the love wherewith thou hast loved me may be in them, and I in them.

Chapter 18

¹When Jesus had spoken these words, he went forth with his disciples over the brook Cedron, where was a garden, into the which he entered, and his disciples.

²And Judas also, which betrayed him, knew the place: for Jesus ofttimes resorted thither with his disciples.

³Judas then, having received a band *of men* and officers from the chief priests and Pharisees, cometh thither with lanterns and torches and weapons.

⁴Jesus therefore, knowing all things that should come upon him, went forth, and said unto them, Whom seek ye?

Identified with peace, with joy, with love, we spontaneously move from one expression, one form to another with uninterrupted grace, beauty and thanksgiving.

25. "The natural experience of peace and joy has been fleeting and hidden from humanity for too long. Through our work and discipline here together we bring peace and joy again to its rightful authority in human affairs.

26. "Peace, joy and love are three words for the same living awareness, and this awareness is alive as each of us. It is this aware presence that I have come to magnify, and teach and point to once again so that everyone might remember and reconnect with this, their own first and most natural identity. We share this identity. It is love itself, peace itself, joy itself. We are expressions of that. We are that."

Chapter 18

1. After Jesus and his friends talked in private together about these things, so deeply, clearly and openly, they then walked across the bridge that spanned a small river and into one of the public gardens that was kept there.

2. Jesus and his friends had often come together in this public garden. Judas, Jesus' unhappy and mixed-up friend, also knew that they gathered here often.

3. Judas had reported on Jesus to the elders of the tribe, and so they appointed him head of a crew of armed men who carried torches, spears and ropes. This group of men went to the garden to arrest Jesus.

4. When Jesus saw them coming, he knew what was happening. He went forward to meet them. "Who are you looking for?" Jesus asked, though he already knew the answer.

⁵They answered him, Jesus of Nazareth. Jesus saith unto them, I am *he*. And Judas also, which betrayed him, stood with them.

⁶As soon then as he had said unto them, I am *he*, they went backward, and fell to the ground.

⁷Then asked he them again, Whom seek ye? And they said, Jesus of Nazareth.

⁸Jesus answered, I have told you that I am *he*: if therefore ye seek me, let these go their way:

⁹That the saying might be fulfilled, which he spake, Of them which thou gavest me have I lost none.

¹⁰Then Simon Peter having a sword drew it, and smote the high priest's servant, and cut off his right ear. The servant's name was Malchus.

¹¹Then said Jesus unto Peter, Put up thy sword into the sheath: the cup which my Father hath given me, shall I not drink it?

¹²Then the band and the captain and officers of the Jews took Jesus, and bound him,

¹³And led him away to Annas first; for he was father in law to Caiaphas, which was the high priest that same year.

5. "We're looking for Jesus," they said. Judas was standing with the crew, but wasn't saying anything. "I am Jesus," Jesus said.

6. Curiously, Jesus' simple statement of his human name released a powerful wave of energy and recognition through the group who had come to arrest him. With Jesus' words, they all spontaneously moved back many steps. Some of them actually fell to the ground.

7. Again, Jesus asked them, "Who did you say you were looking for?" And again one of the leaders said, "Jesus."

8. "I already told you, I am Jesus," said Jesus "Since I am the one you're looking for, you can let the rest of these folks go on home."

9. Again, this was a demonstration of how peace and joy watches out for and protects its own highest expression.

10. But Peter, one of Jesus' best friends, didn't want these men to take Jesus. Peter pulled out his sword and swung it at one of the men there, who had been helping the crew's leaders. Peter's sword sliced off the man's ear.

11. Jesus put up his hand. "Peter, put your sword down. Love itself is unfolding here. This ancient presence is much more powerful than any sword. Would you have me not follow love?" And then Jesus picked up the man's ear, talked to the man quietly, and then gently held the ear to the man's head. The ear reattached as it had originally been.

12. But the gang of men were frightened and didn't want to see any more of Jesus' healings. They moved in and quickly took him and bound him with ropes.

13. They then walked him to the meeting hall to appear before one of the tribal elders, who happened to be the

¹⁴Now Caiaphas was he, which gave counsel to the Jews, that it was expedient that one man should die for the people.

¹⁵And Simon Peter followed Jesus, and *so did* another disciple: that disciple was known unto the high priest, and went in with Jesus into the palace of the high priest.

¹⁶But Peter stood at the door without. Then went out that other disciple, which was known unto the high priest, and spake unto her that kept the door, and brought in Peter.

¹⁷Then saith the damsel that kept the door unto Peter, Art not thou also *one* of this man's disciples? He saith, I am not.

¹⁸And the servants and officers stood there, who had made a fire of coals; for it was cold: and they warmed themselves: and Peter stood with them, and warmed himself.

¹⁹The high priest then asked Jesus of his disciples, and of his doctrine.

²⁰Jesus answered him, I spake openly to the world; I ever taught in the synagogue, and in the temple, whither the Jews always resort; and in secret have I said nothing.

father-in-law of Caiaphus, who was in charge of the hall.

14. Caiaphus had previously suggested to the rest of the tribe that in order to keep the peace and to keep good relations with the civil authorities it would be better that they sacrifice and make an example of one person so that the political pressure would be off the rest of them.

15. Peter and another of Jesus' friends followed the group of men who had taken Jesus to the meeting hall. The other friend was already known by many of the people at the meeting hall so he was allowed to go in with Jesus.

16. Peter though, had to wait outside, by the front door. Peter's friend, seeing what happened, came back and talked to the woman keeping watch at the door. The friend told the woman that Peter was okay, that he was with him, and should be allowed into the meeting hall.

17. The woman looked at Peter and asked him, "Aren't you a friend of Jesus, that man they just arrested?" Peter was suddenly afraid. He denied it, said no, he wasn't a friend, that he was just passing through.

18. Then, rather than going inside the meeting hall, Peter turned and went to join a group of men who were warming themselves around a fire because it had grown cold. The men were soldiers and those who were employed to serve the soldiers. Peter was hoping to blend in so he joined the group standing around the fire.

19. Back in the meeting hall, the leader of the tribe asked Jesus about his friends, and what it was that he was secretly teaching.

20. Jesus reminded the leader that what he had been teaching was no secret. He had been teaching openly, in this very meeting hall, and in the market, and wherever the tribe was gathered. What he taught in private about

²¹Why askest thou me? ask them which heard me, what I have said unto them: behold, they know what I said.

²²And when he had thus spoken, one of the officers which stood by struck Jesus with the palm of his hand, saying, Answerest thou the high priest so?

²³Jesus answered him, If I have spoken evil, bear witness of the evil: but if well, why smitest thou me?

²⁴Now Annas had sent him bound unto Caiaphas the high priest.

²⁵And Simon Peter stood and warmed himself. They said therefore unto him, Art not thou also *one* of his disciples? He denied *it*, and said, I am not.

²⁶One of the servants of the high priest, being *his* kinsman whose ear Peter cut off, saith, Did not I see thee in the garden with him?

²⁷Peter then denied again: and immediately the cock crew.

²⁸Then led they Jesus from Caiaphas unto the hall of judgment: and it was early; and they themselves went not into the judgment hall, lest they should be defiled; but that they might eat the passover.

Chapter Eighteen: Love Is More Powerful than The Sword

joy and peace and awareness was the same thing he taught publicly.

21. Jesus encouraged the man who was questioning him to ask the people what it was that he was teaching. The people now knew his teachings quite well.

22. One of the leader's henchman, who had been listening, stepped forward and said to Jesus, "Don't get smart with him. Answer him directly. Who do you think you are?" The henchman was holding a small whip in his hand, moving it back and forth in a menacing manner.

23. Jesus, unafraid, looked at the man compassionately. "I speak whatever joy prompts me to speak," Jesus said calmly. "If what I said is untrue or offensive, say so. Otherwise, why do you threaten me?"

24. Back at the fire, one of the men there had seen Jesus tied up and taken away to the leaders in the meeting hall.

25. He looked at Peter and asked, "Aren't you one of Jesus' friends? One of those who had been following him around?" Peter was feeling more and more threatened. "No, no I'm not," Peter said. "That wasn't me."

26. But one of the men standing there happened to be the same man whose ear Peter had cut off, and who Jesus had then healed. "Yes you are, " the man said to Peter. "I was there. I saw you with him. It was you, I'm almost certain."

27. "No, no, that wasn't me," Peter said again. And when he said these words, a rooster crowed, and then Peter remembered Jesus' telling him that before the sun came up Peter would deny he even knew him three different times.

28. Back in the meeting hall, the leader had his henchmen take Jesus away, and lock him in the room that they used

[29] Pilate then went out unto them, and said, What accusation bring ye against this man?

[30] They answered and said unto him, If he were not a malefactor, we would not have delivered him up unto thee.

[31] Then said Pilate unto them, Take ye him, and judge him according to your law. The Jews therefore said unto him, It is not lawful for us to put any man to death:

[32] That the saying of Jesus might be fulfilled, which he spake, signifying what death he should die.

[33] Then Pilate entered into the judgment hall again, and called Jesus, and said unto him, Art thou the King of the Jews?

[34] Jesus answered him, Sayest thou this thing of thyself, or did others tell it thee of me?

[35] Pilate answered, Am I a Jew? Thine own nation and the chief priests have delivered thee unto me: what hast thou done?

[36] Jesus answered, My kingdom is not of this world: if my kingdom were of this world, then would my servants fight, that I should not be delivered to the Jews: but now is my kingdom not from hence.

for trials and sentencing. The men who locked him up didn't stay with him because it was the day and time for them to attend to their traditional tribal rituals. They were anxious to leave to go perform these mandatory rites.

29. Pontius Pilate was the military governor of the region, and was also responsible for collecting taxes and appointing local officials who would make sure the local tribes stayed peaceful and subservient. Pilate was aware of what was happening with Jesus, so he asked the men who had taken him captive, "What's this man's crime? What are you charging him with?"

30. "He's a criminal, a terrorist," the men answered. "He's been doing all kinds of evil in our community. That's why we arrested him, and that's why we brought him to you."

31. "He's from your own tribe," Pilate said. "I don't see what laws of ours he's broken. Take him back and judge him according to your own tribe's laws, and do with him whatever your tradition and custom allows you to do." "We would," the men replied, "but our traditions and customs wouldn't allow us to put him to death. That's something you would have to do. "

32. Jesus had already told his friends on several occasions that the straight-laced members of the tribe wanted to silence him by having him put to death. Now it was apparent to everyone that Jesus had seen this coming.

33. So Pilate went into the room where they were keeping Jesus. They looked each other in the eye. "So," Pilate asked, with a smile, "Seems like you're a trouble maker. Have you decided you should be the new king of your tribe?"

34. Jesus smiled back. "Do you know of anyone, anywhere at any time, that ever heard me say such a thing? Or did

[37] Pilate therefore said unto him, Art thou a king then? Jesus answered, Thou sayest that I am a king. To this end was I born, and for this cause came I into the world, that I should bear witness unto the truth. Every one that is of the truth heareth my voice.

[38] Pilate saith unto him, What is truth? And when he had said this, he went out again unto the Jews, and saith unto them, I find in him no fault *at all*.

[39] But ye have a custom, that I should release unto you one at the passover: will ye therefore that I release unto you the King of the Jews?

[40] Then cried they all again, saying, Not this man, but Barabbas. Now Barabbas was a robber.

Chapter Eighteen: Love Is More Powerful than The Sword

someone just tell you that this is what I wanted, or claimed?"

35. Pilate's smile disappeared and he brusquely answered, "I am not in your tribe. I wouldn't know such a thing. You're here because the elders and officials of your tribe delivered you to me. So what was your crime? What have you done?"

36. "I have shown a natural power and authority that has nothing to do with the political and social powers of the tribe. If my interest was to gain political power then my friends would have fought for me and would not have allowed our tribe's leaders to take me this way. But the power and authority that I have demonstrated is still present, and in no way diminished by my being here."

37. Pilate responded, "So you do see yourself as some kind of authority figure, is that right?" Jesus answered, "Maybe that's how you see me. What I know is that my destiny is to know and share undying joy and peace, because this is my nature. Others hear my words and witness my demonstration and recognize their own nature, their own destiny in this that I am sharing."

38. Pilate just looked at him for a long moment, and then shook his head. "Where can one find joy and peace in this world?" he asked. And then without waiting for an answer turned and left. He went into the other room and told the leaders of the tribe, "I don't see anything wrong with this man.

39. "I know it's your tradition at this particular time of year to release someone who has been arrested, and spare them from punishment, even from death. So should I release this man so he can be the new king of your tribe?"

40. The leaders there who had arranged for Jesus to be arrested were quick to say no, don't release him. Release

Chapter 19

¹Then Pilate therefore took Jesus, and scourged *him*.

²And the soldiers platted a crown of thorns, and put *it* on his head, and they put on him a purple robe,

³And said, Hail, King of the Jews! and they smote him with their hands.

⁴Pilate therefore went forth again, and saith unto them, Behold, I bring him forth to you, that ye may know that I find no fault in him.

⁵Then came Jesus forth, wearing the crown of thorns, and the purple robe. And *Pilate* saith unto them, Behold the man!

⁶When the chief priests therefore and officers saw him, they cried out, saying, Crucify *him*, crucify *him*. Pilate saith unto them, Take ye him, and crucify *him*: for I find no fault in him.

⁷The Jews answered him, We have a law, and by our law he ought to die, because he made himself the Son of God.

someone else – release that fellow who was caught robbing folks and leading a rebellion. The one who was tried and sentenced to death. Release him, the robber, and not Jesus.

Chapter 19

1. Pilate shook his head, and then, bending to the wishes of those elders, ordered that Jesus be beaten and whipped.

2. Pilate's soldiers, making fun of their prisoner, made a crown of thorns, and put an old purple robe on Jesus, pretending that he was a king.

3. "Hooray for the king of the tribe," the soldiers shouted and laughed. And then proceeded, again, to beat him with their hands.

4. Pilate was worried so he went again to the leaders of the tribe and said, "As I told you before, I don't know what that man did wrong. He appears quite innocent to me."

5. Jesus, wearing the crown of thorns and the purple robe, was brought into the room with Pilate and the elders. Pilate saw him and exclaimed, "Here, look, here's your man!"

6. When the elders saw Jesus they were a bit frightened. "Execute him ," the leaders whispered. "Put him to death, quickly." Pilate responded, again, "You people take him. You people put him to death. I already told you I can't find anything he did wrong."

7. The men from the tribe answered, "We have strict traditions and rituals that everyone must follow in our tribe. And according to our traditions he must be put to death because he claimed he himself was the physical embodiment of all life and love and peace and joy."

⁸When Pilate therefore heard that saying, he was the more afraid;

⁹And went again into the judgment hall, and saith unto Jesus, Whence art thou? But Jesus gave him no answer.

¹⁰Then saith Pilate unto him, Speakest thou not unto me? knowest thou not that I have power to crucify thee, and have power to release thee?

¹¹Jesus answered, Thou couldest have no power *at all* against me, except it were given thee from above: therefore he that delivered me unto thee hath the greater sin.

¹²And from thenceforth Pilate sought to release him: but the Jews cried out, saying, If thou let this man go, thou art not Caesar's friend: whosoever maketh himself a king speaketh against Caesar.

¹³When Pilate therefore heard that saying, he brought Jesus forth, and sat down in the judgment seat in a place that is called the Pavement, but in the Hebrew, Gabbatha.

¹⁴And it was the preparation of the passover, and about the sixth hour: and he saith unto the Jews, Behold your King!

¹⁵But they cried out, Away with *him*, away with *him*, crucify him. Pilate saith unto them, Shall I crucify your King? The chief priests answered, We have no king but Caesar.

8. Pilate himself couldn't understand how any man could make such a claim, and suddenly he too was frightened.

9. Pilate had Jesus taken into the judgment room again and asked him, "Who exactly are you? And what are you really claiming to be?" This time Jesus just remained quiet.

10. Jesus' silence made Pilate mad. "Man, don't you know who I am?" Pilate asked him. "Don't you realize that I have the power to either put you to death or let you go?"

11. Jesus answered, "The power that controls my destiny is the power of love, of joy and peace. We would not be here together, in the circumstances that we are in today, unless love, joy and peace had brought me here for its own purposes. You have no power over love."

12. Jesus' words convinced Pilate, and relaxed him, so he again went to the elders and told them they should release this man. But the elders of the tribe refused. They told Pilate that if he let Jesus go that meant he was not fulfilling his duties as the governor of this state. They reminded Pilate that this man was claiming to have power greater than the state and yet Pilate was willing to let him go. If Pilate let him go, they said, it would clearly demonstrate that Pilate was no longer competent to be the governor.

13. Pilate sighed, said okay. He ordered Jesus to be taken to the court where Pilate sat and gave out his official orders and judgments.

14. It was the day before another of the main tribal celebrations. Pilate was frustrated with the tribe. When Jesus came in, he said to them, "Here's your leader. Take a good look at your king."

15. "He's not our king, he's not our leader," they replied. "You and your leaders are our leaders. So put him to

¹⁶Then delivered he him therefore unto them to be crucified. And they took Jesus, and led *him* away.

¹⁷And he bearing his cross went forth into a place called *the place* of a skull, which is called in the Hebrew Golgotha:

¹⁸Where they crucified him, and two other with him, on either side one, and Jesus in the midst.

¹⁹And Pilate wrote a title, and put *it* on the cross. And the writing was, JESUS OF NAZARETH THE KING OF THE JEWS.

²⁰This title then read many of the Jews: for the place where Jesus was crucified was nigh to the city: and it was written in Hebrew, *and* Greek, *and* Latin.

²¹Then said the chief priests of the Jews to Pilate, Write not, The King of the Jews; but that he said, I am King of the Jews.

²²Pilate answered, What I have written I have written.

²³Then the soldiers, when they had crucified Jesus, took his garments, and made four parts, to every soldier a part; and also *his* coat: now the coat was without seam, woven from the top throughout.

death. We've had enough of him. Away with him. Crucify him, and quickly."

16. Pilate just shook his head, finally agreed to the tribal leaders' demand, and waved them off. So the officers and soldiers took Jesus away to killed by crucifixion.

17. They gave Jesus a cross, onto which he would be hung. They made him carry it outside the city's walls to the hill where the hanging of prisoners took place.

18. At the hill, they nailed Jesus's flesh to the cross he had been carrying. They then placed the cross upright so he would hang. Two other prisoners were also there that day being hung.

19. Pilate was still upset with the tribe for insisting on this, so he had a sign made that read, "Jesus of Nazareth, King of the Tribe." He had the sign placed on top of his cross.

20. Pilate had the sign written in three different languages, so that anybody coming by could read it, or have it read to them if they couldn't read. Since the place of the hanging was just outside the city's walls, many people read the signs.

21. The signs bothered the elders of the tribe. "He's not the king of our tribe," they complained to Pilate. "He claimed to be king but he wasn't. You shouldn't keep those signs up there, because they aren't accurate."

22. Pilate answered, "The signs stay. They say exactly what I wanted them to say."

23. Because they loved him, Jesus' friends had given him an expensive, well-made robe and coat woven from the highest quality material. The soldiers who had taken part in Jesus' hanging now took the coat with the intention of cutting it into four pieces to give out as souvenirs for what

²⁴They said therefore among themselves, Let us not rend it, but cast lots for it, whose it shall be: that the scripture might be fulfilled, which saith, They parted my raiment among them, and for my vesture they did cast lots. These things therefore the soldiers did.

²⁵Now there stood by the cross of Jesus his mother, and his mother's sister, Mary the *wife* of Cleophas, and Mary Magdalene.

²⁶When Jesus therefore saw his mother, and the disciple standing by, whom he loved, he saith unto his mother, Woman, behold thy son!

²⁷Then saith he to the disciple, Behold thy mother! And from that hour that disciple took her unto his own *home*.

²⁸After this, Jesus knowing that all things were now accomplished, that the scripture might be fulfilled, saith, I thirst.

²⁹Now there was set a vessel full of vinegar: and they filled a spunge with vinegar, and put *it* upon hyssop, and put *it* to his mouth.

³⁰When Jesus therefore had received the vinegar, he said, It is finished: and he bowed his head, and gave up the ghost.

Chapter Nineteen: Love Is the Highest Power

they had done.

24. But before they cut the robe, the soldiers started joking amongst themselves. "Hey let's throw the dice to see who gets this," one of them said. "The tradition of their tribe says that when the king comes, he has prophesied that the soldiers will cast dice to see who gets his robe." They laughed and threw the dice.

25. Jesus' mother, Mary, had come to where he was hung, along with her sister, and a young woman friend named Mary Magdalene.

26. When Jesus saw his mother he smiled faintly, and nodded his head. "Mother, don't worry. You have given birth to new forms of happiness for the whole world"

27. And to Mary Magdalene, Jesus said, "She is the mother of happiness. Treat her as such." And from that day, not only Mary Magdalene but all the friends cared for and cherished Jesus' mother in the way she deserved, and every mother deserves.

28. Jesus knew his work in the physical body was complete. He was very aware of the traditions of the tribe, so in accordance with the traditions, he called to those near by. "This physical form with which I am still associated needs water." Jesus knew what their response would be.

29. A pot of vinegar was nearby. The soldiers, still joking amongst themselves, dipped a sponge into the pot of vinegar and then squeezed the sponge out onto some mint leaves and put the leaves to Jesus' mouth.

30. When Jesus tasted the leaves soaked in vinegar, he knew this was the sign that his work in the physical body was complete. He looked at the crowd gathered there and smiled. "It's over," he said softly, then sighed, took in then

³¹The Jews therefore, because it was the preparation, that the bodies should not remain upon the cross on the sabbath day, (for that sabbath day was an high day,) besought Pilate that their legs might be broken, and *that* they might be taken away.

³²Then came the soldiers, and brake the legs of the first, and of the other which was crucified with him.

³³But when they came to Jesus, and saw that he was dead already, they brake not his legs:

³⁴But one of the soldiers with a spear pierced his side, and forthwith came there out blood and water.

³⁵And he that saw *it* bare record, and his record is true: and he knoweth that he saith true, that ye might believe.

³⁶For these things were done, that the scripture should be fulfilled, A bone of him shall not be broken.

³⁷And again another scripture saith, They shall look on him whom they pierced.

let out a long last breath. He did not breathe in again. His head fell, and he was no longer in the body.

31. In the tradition of the tribe it was deemed unlucky and bad form to have prisoners who had been hung still hanging there on the holy day, which was coming up that weekend. So the tribal leaders went to Pilate and asked if all three prisoners could be taken down—and for good measure, their legs broken to make sure they wouldn't cause any more trouble and would die in short order.

32. Pilate agreed to the request so the soldiers came and took down the two who were hanging with Jesus and broke their legs.

33. When they came to Jesus, however, it was clear to the soldiers that he was already dead and that therefore they didn't need to break his legs.

34. Just to make sure, however, one of the soldiers took out his spear and speared Jesus in the side. Blood and water came out of the wound, but Jesus hadn't flinched.

35. All of these events were witnessed and verified by many people, so that the people who followed could know what happened and trust the record.

36. Most of the people who took part in these events did not realize that they were actually fulfilling prophesy and tradition by their actions. For instance, the tribe's tradition and prophesy had said that when the new king came, he would do the things that Jesus had done, and when he left, he would leave in tact, without a bone ever being broken.

37. Another example of prophesy being fulfilled was the saying that they would look on the king "who had been pierced." Jesus' wound in the side fulfilled that prophesy.

³⁸And after this Joseph of Arimathaea, being a disciple of Jesus, but secretly for fear of the Jews, besought Pilate that he might take away the body of Jesus: and Pilate gave *him* leave. He came therefore, and took the body of Jesus.

³⁹And there came also Nicodemus, which at the first came to Jesus by night, and brought a mixture of myrrh and aloes, about an hundred pound *weight*.

⁴⁰Then took they the body of Jesus, and wound it in linen clothes with the spices, as the manner of the Jews is to bury.

⁴¹Now in the place where he was crucified there was a garden; and in the garden a new sepulchre, wherein was never man yet laid.

⁴²There laid they Jesus therefore because of the Jews' preparation *day*; for the sepulchre was nigh at hand.

Chapter 20

¹The first *day* of the week cometh Mary Magdalene early, when it was yet dark, unto the sepulchre, and seeth the stone taken away from the sepulchre.

²Then she runneth, and cometh to Simon Peter, and to the other disciple, whom Jesus loved, and saith unto them, They have taken away the Lord out of the sepulchre, and we know not where they have laid him.

³⁸. One of the local rich men, who was afraid of the tribe's elders but was secretly a friend and follower of Jesus, went in private to Pilate and asked him if he might take Jesus' body away, and seal it up in the tomb that he had actually bought and prepared for himself. Pilate gave the rich man permission, so the man arranged for Jesus' body to be taken away to the tomb.

³⁹. Before they took him away another of Jesus' good friends came in the secret of night with a large quantity of high quality incense and precious oils which they used to cover and prepare Jesus' body for burial.

⁴⁰. His friends spread the oils and incense over Jesus' body and then wrapped the body in linens, as was the custom of the tribe in preparing a body for burial.

⁴¹. The rich man's burial tomb, which had never been used, was located on a hillside in a quiet garden near where the hangings had occurred.

⁴². So his friends took Jesus' body and laid it in the tomb. They then had a large boulder placed in front of it to seal it up. According to the tribe's tradition and ritual, this all needed to be done before the holy days arrived

Chapter 20

¹. Several days later, after the holy days had passed, Mary Magdalene, Jesus' good friend came to the tomb in the early hours, before the sun was up. She was surprised when she saw that the rock had been taken away from the entrance.

². She turned and quickly ran to where Peter and another of Jesus' good friends were staying. "They've taken our dear friend's body out of the tomb," she cried. "I have no idea what they've done with it."

³Peter therefore went forth, and that other disciple, and came to the sepulchre.

⁴So they ran both together: and the other disciple did outrun Peter, and came first to the sepulchre.

⁵And he stooping down, *and looking in*, saw the linen clothes lying; yet went he not in.

⁶Then cometh Simon Peter following him, and went into the sepulchre, and seeth the linen clothes lie,

⁷And the napkin, that was about his head, not lying with the linen clothes, but wrapped together in a place by itself.

⁸Then went in also that other disciple, which came first to the sepulchre, and he saw, and believed.

⁹For as yet they knew not the scripture, that he must rise again from the dead.

¹⁰Then the disciples went away again unto their own home.

¹¹But Mary stood without at the sepulchre weeping: and as she wept, she stooped down, *and looked* into the sepulchre,

¹²And seeth two angels in white sitting, the one at the head, and the other at the feet, where the body of Jesus had lain.

¹³And they say unto her, Woman, why weepest thou? She saith unto them, Because they have taken away my Lord, and I know not where they have laid him.

Chapter Twenty: Your Peace Is Closer than Your Breath

³· Hearing this, Peter and the other friend rushed out toward the tomb. Mary followed.

⁴· The friend was faster, and ran ahead of Peter and Mary and arrived there first.

⁵. He looked into the tomb and saw Jesus' burial linens folded neatly on the burial bench, but Jesus was nowhere to be found. The friend was a bit too frightened and superstitious to go into the tomb itself.

⁶· Peter arrived shortly after this. Peter was not afraid. He walked into the tomb to examine the burial linens.

⁷. Peter saw the linens, and then saw the traditional head cloth neatly folded in a different corner all by itself.

⁸· The other friend, seeing Peter's boldness, then also went into the tomb and saw what Peter had seen.

⁹. Neither Peter nor the friend were yet aware that this would be yet another demonstration of the power of joy, the power of peace, that Jesus had come to share. Nor were they yet aware of the tribe's traditional prophesy that their new king would be able to overcome death itself.

¹⁰· So Peter and his friend left the tomb and returned home.

¹¹· By this time, however, Mary had arrived, and she was not ready or willing to leave. She was crying outside the tomb. Then she too, although remaining outside, stooped down to look inside.

¹². There, inside the tomb, Mary saw two bright radiances, one at the head where Jesus had been lain, and one at the foot.

¹³.And then from the radiances, she heard a clear voice ask, "Friend, why are you crying?" She answered them saying,

¹⁴And when she had thus said, she turned herself back, and saw Jesus standing, and knew not that it was Jesus.

¹⁵Jesus saith unto her, Woman, why weepest thou? whom seekest thou? She, supposing him to be the gardener, saith unto him, Sir, if thou have borne him hence, tell me where thou hast laid him, and I will take him away.

¹⁶Jesus saith unto her, Mary. She turned herself, and saith unto him, Rabboni; which is to say, Master.

¹⁷Jesus saith unto her, Touch me not; for I am not yet ascended to my Father: but go to my brethren, and say unto them, I ascend unto my Father, and your Father; and *to* my God, and your God.

¹⁸Mary Magdalene came and told the disciples that she had seen the Lord, and *that* he had spoken these things unto her.

¹⁹Then the same day at evening, being the first *day* of the week, when the doors were shut where the disciples were assembled for fear of the Jews, came Jesus and stood in the midst, and saith unto them, Peace *be* unto you.

"Because they have taken away the body of my teacher, who was also my very good and wondrous friend. I don't know where they took him."

14. And then Mary felt someone standing behind her. She turned from the tomb and there was Jesus, though she didn't recognize him because he glowed and was so fresh.

15. Jesus smiled and said, "Friend, why are you crying? And who are you looking for?" Mary assumed that this was one of the groundskeepers, or one of the gardeners. "Sir," she said, "if you were the one who took him away, or know who did and where they put him, please tell me. I will go and get him. I won't be any more trouble for you."

16. Again Jesus smiled, and simply said, "Mary." Immediately Mary recognized him, and this time burst into tears of joy. "My love, my joy, my peace," she said, opening her arms to him and started to move in his direction.

17. Jesus smiled and held up his hand. "I'm here for you, and with you, though not yet to be touched with hands," he said. "I am in the process of releasing the last vestiges of any appearance of separation from objectless peace, pure love, objectless joy. So go and tell our friends that I am now peace itself, love itself, joy itself, and that they will find me when they turn to their own peace and joy."

18. Mary nodded her head and then ran to tell her friends that she had seen Jesus and he had told her these things.

19. That evening the friends came together to discuss all the recent events. They were meeting secretly in a room with the doors closed because they were still frightened about what the tribal leaders might do to them. As they were talking, Jesus was suddenly somehow there in the midst of

[20] And when he had so said, he shewed unto them *his* hands and his side. Then were the disciples glad, when they saw the Lord.

[21] Then said Jesus to them again, Peace *be* unto you: as *my* Father hath sent me, even so send I you.

[22] And when he had said this, he breathed on *them*, and saith unto them, Receive ye the Holy Ghost:

[23] Whose soever sins ye remit, they are remitted unto them; *and* whose soever *sins* ye retain, they are retained.

[24] But Thomas, one of the twelve, called Didymus, was not with them when Jesus came.

[25] The other disciples therefore said unto him, We have seen the Lord. But he said unto them, Except I shall see in his hands the print of the nails, and put my finger into the print of the nails, and thrust my hand into his side, I will not believe.

Chapter Twenty: Your Peace Is Closer than Your Breath

them. He smiled at them. "Peace be with you," he said, holding up his hand.

[20]. His friends didn't understand what was happening here. So Jesus held out both his hands, to show the wounds where he had been nailed to the cross. And then he moved his robe aside to show where the soldier had pierced him with a sword. And now his friends were happy and relieved and rejoicing, knowing it was really him.

[21.] And again, Jesus said to them, "Peace, friends, be with you. Joy, peace and love have sent me to you. Now I send you with joy, peace and love into the world."

[22].Jesus took a deep breath, and let it out. "Your joy, your peace, your love," he said, "Is closer even than your breath. It belongs to no one, and yet it is everyone's.

[23]."Your work with the people you meet in the world is to dissolve their unhappiness, to share your joy and peace and love, that they might likewise recognize their own joy and peace and love. All you can do is remain in your own peace and joy wherever you are. Some people will recognize the gift you have to offer, and some won't. Either way, simply remain in your peace and joy."

[24]. Not all of Jesus' friends, of course, including Thomas, one of his closest friends, were present at this wonderful reunion with him.

[25]. When the friends told Thomas about their meeting, Thomas couldn't help but doubt their stories. He had personally witnessed Jesus death on the cross. "I would need to see him for myself," Thomas said. "And not only would I need to see him, I would need to see his hands and put my finger into the wounds where they nailed him up and put my hand into the wound in his side where they speared him. Then, maybe, I would believe."

²⁶And after eight days again his disciples were within, and Thomas with them: *then* came Jesus, the doors being shut, and stood in the midst, and said, Peace *be* unto you.

²⁷Then saith he to Thomas, Reach hither thy finger, and behold my hands; and reach hither thy hand, and thrust *it* into my side: and be not faithless, but believing.

²⁸And Thomas answered and said unto him, My Lord and my God.

²⁹Jesus saith unto him, Thomas, because thou hast seen me, thou hast believed: blessed *are* they that have not seen, and *yet* have believed.

³⁰And many other signs truly did Jesus in the presence of his disciples, which are not written in this book:

³¹But these are written, that ye might believe that Jesus is the Christ, the Son of God; and that believing ye might have life through his name.

26. Eight days later the friends were again gathered in the same room, with the doors closed. This time Thomas was among those who had come together. And once again, Jesus somehow mysteriously was there with them, without the door being opened. And once again he smiled at them and said, "Peace be with you, friends."

27. He turned to Thomas. "Friend," Jesus said, holding out his hand. "Here, put your finger into my palm, like you said you wanted to do, and feel the wound. And with your other hand, feel the wound in my side, and know that it is truly me. Don't doubt your joy, my friend. Don't doubt your peace. Trust them, as I have encouraged you to do."

28. Thomas was immediately convinced. He didn't have to touch Jesus' wounds to understand what was happening here and believe his words. "Oh my brother," Thomas said. "You have shown me beyond doubt that you are undying love and peace and joy."

29. Jesus smiled at him. "Now that you've seen me in the flesh, you're convinced. That's as it should be. But countless others have not seen me in the flesh like this and yet have understood my teachings and have begun to practice my simple ways. Their happiness will continue to grow and strengthen throughout their lives."

30. After Jesus' return from the tomb many other wonderful healings and beautiful events and miraculous appearances took place among Jesus' friends that are not recorded here in this report.

31. Those events that are recorded here are offered so that others who read this might understand the teachings that Jesus shared and the peaceable way of life he encouraged. Jesus was and is awareness itself, peace itself, love itself. Those who recognize their own joy and honor it will find him in it, and through this living joy life will progressively unfold in peaceable and harmonious ways.

Chapter 21

¹After these things Jesus shewed himself again to the disciples at the sea of Tiberias; and on this wise shewed he *himself*.

²There were together Simon Peter, and Thomas called Didymus, and Nathanael of Cana in Galilee, and the *sons* of Zebedee, and two other of his disciples.

³Simon Peter saith unto them, I go a fishing. They say unto him, We also go with thee. They went forth, and entered into a ship immediately; and that night they caught nothing.

⁴But when the morning was now come, Jesus stood on the shore: but the disciples knew not that it was Jesus.

⁵Then Jesus saith unto them, Children, have ye any meat? They answered him, No.

⁶And he said unto them, Cast the net on the right side of the ship, and ye shall find. They cast therefore, and now they were not able to draw it for the multitude of fishes.

⁷Therefore that disciple whom Jesus loved saith unto Peter, It is the Lord. Now when Simon Peter heard that it was the Lord, he girt *his* fisher's coat *unto him*, (for he was naked,) and did cast himself into the sea.

Chapter 21

1. In addition to these recently mentioned events, another place that Jesus appeared to his friends after the crucifixion was at the seaside which lay west of the main city.

2. Peter was there, and Thomas and Nathanial and four or five other men who had been Jesus' friends.

3. Peter told the others that he didn't know what to do so he was going back to his old job, and start fishing again. The others said they would join him because it appeared as though the events surrounding Jesus had come to an end. It was time to get back to their old daily routines. So they all went onto their boat, shoved out and fished all day. But by that evening they had caught nothing.

4. They pulled their boat back into the bay, but still off a ways from the shore. They slept on the boat that night. In the morning Jesus was standing on the shore, though they didn't recognize him, since they weren't expecting him.

5. Jesus called out to them, "Brothers, have you caught anything? Do you have anything to eat?" They shook their heads and answered no.

6. He called to them again, "Throw your nets over on the right side of your boat, and you'll do well." They didn't have anything to lose, so they threw their nets onto the right side of the boat, and immediately their nets were brimming with more fish than they could lift.

7. As they were struggling with the overloaded nets, they looked again back at the man standing on the shore. One of the men who had been an especially close friend of Jesus said to Peter, "It's him, it's our friend, our teacher, our brother." Peter looked up, and recognized him. He immediately grabbed his robe, threw it over his head, and then jumped out of the boat to go be with Jesus.

⁸And the other disciples came in a little ship; (for they were not far from land, but as it were two hundred cubits,) dragging the net with fishes.

⁹As soon then as they were come to land, they saw a fire of coals there, and fish laid thereon, and bread.

¹⁰Jesus saith unto them, Bring of the fish which ye have now caught.

¹¹Simon Peter went up, and drew the net to land full of great fishes, an hundred and fifty and three: and for all there were so many, yet was not the net broken.

¹²Jesus saith unto them, Come *and* dine. And none of the disciples durst ask him, Who art thou? knowing that it was the Lord.

¹³Jesus then cometh, and taketh bread, and giveth them, and fish likewise.

¹⁴This is now the third time that Jesus shewed himself to his disciples, after that he was risen from the dead.

¹⁵So when they had dined, Jesus saith to Simon Peter, Simon, *son* of Jonas, lovest thou me more than these? He saith unto him, Yea, Lord; thou knowest that I love thee. He saith unto him, Feed my lambs.

¹⁶He saith to him again the second time, Simon, *son* of Jonas, lovest thou me? He saith unto him, Yea, Lord; thou knowest that I love thee. He saith unto him, Feed my sheep.

Chapter Twenty-One: Teach Others This Joy

8. The others maneuvered the boat toward the shore, which was a hundred yards or so away. They dragged the nets of fish with them.

9. As they approached the shore, they saw a small fire had been made with a handful of fish laid over the coals. And on a nearby stump were some loaves of bread.

10. Jesus smiled at the men in the boat. "Bring up the fish that you have caught," he said.

11. Peter went to help the men in the boat. They pulled the net up—it was the largest catch they had ever caught. Previously, if they had caught even half as many fish, parts of the net would have broken, losing some of the fish. This time, though, the net held, and all of the fish were taken.

12. After the fish were landed, Jesus said to his friends, "Come, eat." Although Jesus' presence was a miracle in itself, none of his friends needed to ask him who he was, because it was obvious to all that he was here, again, with them.

13. Jesus acted as host, and broke apart the loaves of bread and handed them out. Then he likewise took the fish and served them to his friends.

14. This was the third time that this group of friends had been with Jesus since his death and resurrection.

15. After they had eaten, Jesus turned to Peter and asked, "Old friend, do you know me, are you at peace with me, and do you love me?" Peter said, "Yes, of course, you know I do." Jesus nodded and said, "Teach others, then, not only through your words but by your very presence, this way of living that I have taught you."

16. Peter nodded his head. There was a pause. And then Jesus asked a second time, "So you really do know me, and

¹⁷He saith unto him the third time, Simon, *son* of Jonas, lovest thou me? Peter was grieved because he said unto him the third time, Lovest thou me? And he said unto him, Lord, thou knowest all things; thou knowest that I love thee. Jesus saith unto him, Feed my sheep.

¹⁸Verily, verily, I say unto thee, When thou wast young, thou girdedst thyself, and walkedst whither thou wouldest: but when thou shalt be old, thou shalt stretch forth thy hands, and another shall gird thee, and carry *thee* whither thou wouldest not.

¹⁹This spake he, signifying by what death he should glorify God. And when he had spoken this, he saith unto him, Follow me.

Chapter Twenty-One: Teach Others This Joy

are at peace with me, and love me and the simple ways of living that I have taught?" Again Peter said, "Yes, yes, of course I do. I love you, and everything you have taught us and showed to us." Then Jesus said, "People are hungry for the peace and joy that has been demonstrated. So feed them, friend. That is your job, that is your work."

17. Peter was so moved, he was speechless. He just nodded his head in agreement. And then again, after another pause, Jesus asked a third time. "So you do know me, that I am awareness, that I am joy itself, and you love me and are at peace with me?" Peter was disturbed that Jesus kept coming back to him, asking him the same question. "I know you can see into my thoughts and into my feelings, " Peter said. "I know you see into everything in everyone," Peter replied. "So you know I love you, and want to be with you, stand with you, follow the teachings that you have shared." Jesus smiled, and again said, "So teach others, Peter, these things that I have taught you. Love them, and be at peace with them, as I have loved you and am at peace with you." At the time, Peter did not realize that when Jesus now asked him three times about his love and faith and understanding in this way, that Jesus was doing him a deep favor, canceling and healing Peter's three denials right before Jesus' death. And it was not only for Peter that Jesus did this, but for all those who came later, who would likewise deny Jesus and his teachings.

18. "The body goes through its seasons of youth, middle age and old age," Jesus said. "Eventually it grows frail and falls way. Yet, awareness, joy, peace, does not age, does not grow frail, does not fall away. Your true nature, your first identity is not with the body, but with awareness itself, peace itself. This is what I have come to teach and demonstrate and it is what you, too, can teach and demonstrate."

19. Jesus here showed Peter and his other friends, and all those who were to come later, the most simple, natural and

²⁰Then Peter, turning about, seeth the disciple whom Jesus loved following; which also leaned on his breast at supper, and said, Lord, which is he that betrayeth thee?

²¹Peter seeing him saith to Jesus, Lord, and what *shall* this man *do*?

²²Jesus saith unto him, If I will that he tarry till I come, what *is that* to thee? follow thou me.

²³Then went this saying abroad among the brethren, that that disciple should not die: yet Jesus said not unto him, He shall not die; but, If I will that he tarry till I come, what *is that* to thee?

²⁴This is the disciple which testifieth of these things, and wrote these things: and we know that his testimony is true.

²⁵And there are also many other things which Jesus did, the which, if they should be written every one, I suppose that even the world itself could not contain the books that should be written. Amen.

Chapter Twenty-One: Teach Others This Joy

profound way to live —in deliberate, yet natural peace and joy and love. Jesus knew that such practice would lead them to a full, abundant life and humble, loving service until their last days on earth. "Follow the way of joy and peace, Peter," he said again.

20. Peter looked around and saw all of the friends who loved Jesus so deeply, many of whom had been with him through all the days of his teaching. And he knew that Jesus likewise loved them. And then Peter remembered Judas, who had turned Jesus over to the tribal authorities, and then all of the others who had turned against Jesus.

21. "Brother Jesus," Peter said, "What about Judas, and all the others who betrayed you, and led you to the events of these last days. What should we do about them?"

22. Jesus said, "Their own peace, joy waits for them, is available to them, just as it waits for you, and is available to you. Just follow the path that I have shown you. Allow your mind and heart to rest in peace, and all of these other things will naturally take care of themselves."

23. These last words of Jesus were misunderstood by many, who assumed he was saying that those who ignore or betray the principles of joy and peace will suffer no consequences. Yet this is not what Jesus said or meant. He simply implored those who would follow him to always use the guidance of their own love, peace and joy, and that by doing so justice and harmony would naturally be forthcoming from such guidance.

24. This record of Jesus' earthly teachings and demonstrations is offered here by his friends who walked the earth with him, and knew him and loved him and experienced these things first hand.

25. The events and teachings we have here told about regarding our dear friend and teacher are only a small

sampling of the wondrous healings and happy events and miraculous prospering that took place in his presence, not to mention the laughing and singing and dancing that all spontaneously rose up around him. If we were able to write down all of the wonderful things that have occurred because of Jesus' presence here with us, we would cover the entire world with his joyous miracle stories. This is but some of them. Such is joy. Such is peace. Such is life.

                So let it be.

After Word and Invitation

This "happified" Book of John was fun and inspiring to put together. We hope you had fun and were inspired in the reading.

You are invited to contact Bear at:

> Bear Gebhardt, Senior Librarian
> Heart Mountain Monastery
> 606 Hanna St.
> Fort Collins, CO. 80521

e-mail: bear@heartmountainmonastery.com

Or read more about our work, our community and way of life at:

> www.heartmountainmonstary.com

We would love to hear from you.

In peace,

The Friends at Heart Mountain Monastery

"Nobody can bring you peace but yourself."
                 --- Ralph Waldo Emerson

"If someone thinks that love and peace is a cliché that must have been left behind in the Sixties, that's his problem. Love and peace are eternal." --- John Lennon

www.ingramcontent.com/pod-product-compliance
Lightning Source LLC
Chambersburg PA
CBHW070637050426
42451CB00008B/201